The Indispensable Guide to God's Word

Also in the
Indispensable Guide
Series

The Indispensable Guide to Pastoral Care
by Sharyl B. Peterson

The Indispensable Guide to the Old Testament
by Angela Bauer-Levesque

The Indispensable Guide to God's Word

Donald J. Brash

THE
PILGRIM
PRESS
Cleveland

The Pilgrim Press
700 Prospect Avenue
Cleveland, Ohio 44115-1100
thepilgrimpress.com

Biblical quotations are primarily from the New Revised Standard Version of the Bible, © 1989 by the Division of Christian Education of the National Council of the Churches of Christ in the U.S.A., and are used by permission.

Printed in the United Stated of America on acid-free paper that contains post-consumer fiber.

14 13 12 11 10   5 4 3 2

Library of Congress Cataloging-in-Publication Data
Brash, Donald James.
    The indispensable guide to God's Word / Donald J. Brash.
      p. cm.
    Includes bibliographical references.
    ISBN 978-0-8298-1829-1 (alk. paper)
    1. Bible – Criticism, interpretation, etc. I. Title.
BS511.3.B73 2009
220.6'1 – dc22   2009035086

Contents

Preface   vii

Introduction: The Need for Clarity   1

Part I
REVELATION

One   Knowing About   10

Two   Knowing in Person   19

Three   Knowing and Language   28

Part II
INSPIRATION

Four   Stirred Up   40

Five   Stirred by Whom?   49

Six   Stirred How?   61

Part III
CANON

Seven   Telling and Writing   72

Eight   Collections   81

Nine   Authority   90

Part IV
INTERPRETATION

Ten   Incarnation   102

Eleven   Methods   113

Twelve   Application   122

Thirteen   Summary and Conclusion   131

Preface

Pastoral ministry is a calling and a profession with many and varied tasks. Faithfulness in ministry requires faithful attention to the Bible in preaching, as well as in the other arenas of ministry. Whether in the setting of worship, in the classroom, or at Church Bible studies, I have endeavored to interpret the Scriptures responsibly and to apply them in ways that my congregations could readily relate to their daily lives.

This work of biblical interpretation and application is crucial to ministries that take seriously the call to be faithful to Christ in the midst of the sometimes divisive intellectual and ethical issues of our time. As I am sure you have noticed, many of the conflicts that beset our churches are rooted in differing ways of approaching the Bible; differences of biblical interpretation often arise from differing theologies of Scripture.

What I am presenting here is a tool for helping the people of God to understand better the relationship between God and the Bible. It is a book that I hope will equip laypersons, college students, and beginning theological school students to understand how worldviews inform theologies of Scripture, and how one theology of Scripture in particular may strengthen their interpretations. I also am writing to equip thoughtful laypersons to participate in the discussion of theological interpretation that is ongoing in seminaries. Perhaps most importantly, I hope this book better equips lay Christians and aspiring clergy to glean wisdom and guidance from their study of the Bible for navigating the Christian life in our very challenging day and time.

Words of Gratitude

Like books in so many other fields of study, a book of theology may be challenging because of the intellectual complexities that deep thinking involves. But reading a book of theology is unlike reading some other kinds of books because seriously engaging a book of theology involves unique risks. One of these unique risks is that reading a book of theology, especially one on the Bible, involves accepting the possibility that our beliefs and the way we see the world may need to change. If we are willing to learn from one another about Christian faith, then the deepest questions of who we are — our sense of purpose and meaning, our fears, our hopes, our morals, our convictions — will be stirred and questioned by sincere encounters with the beliefs of others.

Simone Weil says well what I am getting at: "It seemed to me certain, and I still think so today, that one can never wrestle enough with God if one does so out of pure regard for the truth. Christ likes us to prefer truth to him because, before being Christ, he is truth. If one turns aside from him to go toward the truth, one will not go far before falling into his arms."[1] I will add that, if I will not seek the truth first, then what I may be holding on to is my own, perhaps inaccurate view of Christ, rather than Christ himself.

If our beliefs change, especially beliefs we have expressed theologically with care, there may be ramifications for our participation in our community of faith. Pastors and teachers, and lay persons too, may find that they are no longer theologically compatible with their community or tradition. One way or another, reading theology involves our own and our community's beliefs. Since our commitment to truth requires us to be honest, we must take the risk that we and our community of faith may need to part ways. The prospect of losing regular contact and support from friends and Church family is unsettling, to say the least; and that is more challenging than intellectual complexities alone would be.

So I thank you from the start for undertaking the risks that are involved in reading this book, laden though those risks are with the promise of growth.

Many other words of thanks are in order. Friends and students have read drafts of parts or all of the developing manuscript of this book. Their insightful conversations and recommendations have contributed immeasurably to the product you have in hand. I cannot name them all, but I would be remiss if I did not mention Ernie Williams, my pastor for several years, and several colleagues: Manfred T. Brauch, Loida Martell-Otero, Benjamin Hartley, George Hancock-Stefan, and Jonathan Malone. In addition to my students in several courses at Palmer Theological Seminary, I received input from an ongoing reading fellowship of American Baptist clergy known affectionately among ourselves as . . . well, perhaps I should not say. My Sunday school class at Medford United Methodist Church discussed some of the ideas I have presented here, and a Church study group at Princeton United Methodist Church, where my lovely and gifted wife, Jana Purkis-Brash, is senior pastor, offered invaluable input and encouragement as they read and discussed the nearly final form of the manuscript. I am grateful to my publisher, Timothy Staveteig of The Pilgrim Press, for this opportunity to write and to publish.

Finally, I dedicate this book to the Reverend Dr. Richard E. Blackwell, the finest of pastor-scholars, whose encouragement, wisdom, and friendship I greatly cherish.

Notes

1. Simone Weil, "Spiritual Autobiography," in *Waiting for God* (New York: Harper Brothers, 1951, 1973), 69. Weil (1909–1943) was a Jewish-Christian philosopher and mystic greatly admired for her political and religious life and thought.

Introduction

The Need for Clarity

A MAJOR DENOMINATION of American Christianity used a slogan a number of years ago that celebrated their identity as "People of The Book."[1] With this slogan they intended to say that they cherish the insight and wisdom they find in the Bible. The members of that denomination do not agree exactly on how the Bible is inspired or on how to interpret it; but they do agree on the centrality of the Bible in guiding their faith and life as God's people.

Since this present book is about "The Book," it is understandably in large measure about the meanings and significance of an array of interrelated words. The words we will consider in the pages ahead enable Christians to express and to explore our beliefs about the Bible. You will recognize, I am sure, the first word on our agenda. It is the word *inerrant*. It may be that you are among those who embrace this word; or you may be among those who think it cannot accurately describe a book with so much humanity about it.

You may have heard statements like, "The Bible says it, I believe it, and it's not up for a debate!" If you have said this or something like it, then you probably believe, as the word *inerrant* suggests, that the Bible is without error. If you are a thoroughgoing inerrantist, then you believe the writers of the Bible wrote truly and accurately not only when they wrote about God and God's will for us, but also when they wrote about history and the natural world; you believe the biblical writers spoke truly and accurately not only when they interpreted the meaning of historical events but also when they described those events; and you believe the biblical writers' interpretations did not distort their accounts of what happened. If you use the word *inerrant* when speaking about

1

the Bible, then the divineness of it is what you most readily see and experience.

On the other hand are those who do not believe we can learn anything reliably true about God or God's will from the Bible. Skeptical moderns and extreme postmoderns hold this point of view. The work of the Jesus Seminar cast doubt on the belief that we can know much at all about the historical Jesus.[2] Extreme postmodern critics doubt that anything universally valid may be drawn from any text, let alone from a text that is supposed to be from God, or the ancient witnesses to God's Incarnation. For these people, the meanings of biblical passages are determined by individuals interpreting them within their communities. Interpretations are subjective and texts have no meaning that certainly applies to all people. If you believe as I have just described, then the humanness of the Bible is what is most apparent to you.

Many of us are between these frequently opposing points of view. We who embrace the mediating position I have in mind affirm with deep conviction the theological trustworthiness of the Bible but do not believe it is without error in matters of science and history.

Those who adopt this mediating position are not surprised or troubled by differences between science and the Bible, nor by differences among related biblical narratives. We are not troubled by these differences because we do not believe God's purpose for the Bible is to teach science or provide precise details about the past. We believe God's Word goes forth for a "purpose, and succeed[s] in the thing for which [God] sent it" (Isa. 55:11). That purpose is *to have a maturing relationship with God as we dialogue with God and one another over the biblical texts.* We embrace the divine inspiration of Scripture, and we see and acknowledge its humanness as well.

The churches I have served have included people across the spectrum of points of view on biblical inspiration and authority. These differing beliefs about the Bible are not petty hair-splitting. Our beliefs about the inspiration and authority of the Bible influence how we interpret it, and our interpretations influence our other beliefs, and with them, our ethics. Differing beliefs about the Bible are often behind Christians' disagreements about whether women should be ordained, or what Holy Communion means, and whether evolution or creationism is correct, to take just three of many examples. Frequently these disagreements come down to different beliefs about how God inspired the Bible and how the authors, scribes, and editors of the Bible may have influenced its contents in their own times and places.

I believe there is a way to understand the Bible's divine inspiration without denying its very human qualities. And conversely, there is a way to fully appreciate the human qualities of the Bible without denying its divine inspiration. But before stating more clearly and explicitly the theology of Scripture I am explaining here, addressing several questions will help us get off to a good start. The first question is, To what exactly am I referring when I say "the Bible"?

The Christian Scriptures

According to Protestant, Roman Catholic, and Orthodox Christians, both the Hebrew Scriptures and the Christian Testament together comprise the Bible.[3] However, not all Christians agree that the writings in the Protestant Bible are all that should be included.

If you look closely at the Bibles in the religion section of a bookstore, you may notice titles in some tables of contents that are not in others. Bibles that were published for Roman Catholic or Orthodox Christians include writings that tradition ascribes to the period between the last of the prophetic books of the Hebrew Scriptures and the first books of the Christian Testament. This collection of works, called the Apocrypha (*apocrypha* is a Greek word meaning "hidden"), is not included in Protestant Bibles. Otherwise, the Bibles of these three great Christian traditions contain the same writings.

When I speak of the Bible, I am thinking of the documents all three traditions embrace in common as Scripture, which is the Bible as Protestants have it. These have been, and still are, the primary sources both for establishing Christian doctrine and for the continuing investigation of Christian theology.

The Bible as Primary Source

Our second preliminary question is this: Why has the Bible been so influential? On a basic, practical level, the answer to this question is not too hard to find.

When you ask questions about the meaning of life, do you go to the Bible for insight? When you need guidance for ethical decisions, do you look to the Bible? Historically, Christians have turned regularly to the Bible, especially regarding the critical issues and passages of life. We do this because we believe that the Bible is where God communicates most clearly and authoritatively about God and God's will for us.

While there is truth and wisdom in the Bible that is recognized even by those who do not believe in God, Christians believe it is not just anyone's truth and wisdom that is revealed to us through the Bible. Christians believe, one way or another, that God had a hand in the Bible's formation. I prefer the image of the shepherd to illustrate this: God shepherded the Scriptures, and God continues to speak authoritatively through them to the hearts and minds of women and men. For this reason above all, the Bible has been consulted and treated as authoritative above other sources as the churches have probed and clarified Christian faith and life. This is why Christians call the Bible "Holy Scripture." It is in this sense most of all that I call it our "primary source."

Our third preliminary question is: When and how did the churches come to the conclusion that God's Word may or should be associated with the Bible? To begin to address this question, we must speak briefly here about the relationship between the Bible and tradition.

The Bible and Tradition

The Bible has been our primary source, but not the only source, of Christian knowledge. Tradition inevitably is involved in our interpretations.

Roman Catholic and Orthodox Christians — and some Protestants, too — very clearly affirm the authority of tradition. While it seems at times to Protestants as though Roman Catholic and Orthodox Christians assign greater authority to tradition than they do to the Bible, we should not conclude that Christians who explicitly hold the value and authority of tradition so highly do not also hold the Bible in high esteem. Catholic and Orthodox churches hold the Bible in very high regard indeed. Following the reading of Scripture in worship, for example, the reader declares that the reading was "the Word of the Lord." The congregation responds with the phrase "thanks be to God." (This liturgical act is common in more than a few Protestant churches too.) The formal teaching of these churches, as seen, for instance, in papal encyclicals, is conscientiously supported through and through by biblical texts and interpretation.

By calling the Bible the *primary* source rather than the *sole* source of Christian theology and ethics, I hope to allow room for recognizing some of the complexities of the relationship between the Bible and tradition, as well as reason and experience. Through this language I hope to allow room for recognizing and embracing the work of the Holy Spirit in biblical formation and interpretation even today. This set of sources — Scripture, tradition, reason, and experience — is popularly called the Wesleyan quadrilateral (named for that energetic founder of Methodism, John Wesley).

Though the Bible continues to be our primary source for knowing God and God's will for humanity, the manner of its divine inspiration, the nature of its authority, and our methods of interpreting it are still debated.

More on Some Current Tensions

If you have been party to debates over the hot-button ethical issues of our time, then you know what I said earlier is true: Differing beliefs about the nature of the Bible and its interpretation stand close to the roots of those arguments. In addition to the three I mentioned earlier are the churches' responses to the legalization of abortion, the effort to use inclusive language in the translating of the Bible and in worship, and the status of homosexual persons in the churches, especially in professional ministry. Indeed, the precise nature of the inspiration and authority of the Bible is itself among the sometimes hotly debated subjects within and among churches today.

The inspiration and authority of the Bible is not only an issue in debates among Christians, it also is a point of contention in inter-religious dialogue and between Christians and atheists. As we all know, there are religions other than Christianity; they too have their sacred books, and atheists are quick to point out the Bible's very human flaws. When persons from other religions, or those who reject religion altogether, think of Christianity, they associate our faith with the Bible. Clarity about how we see our sacred text is critical when discussing our faith with so many people around us.

The Bible and Drama

I assert that the Bible's nature and purpose welcome a lively diversity of interpretations and life-shaping encounters with God and the communion of saints. I also believe that it does so without forcing us to conclude that doctrines and clear ethical standards cannot be drawn from the Bible. Explaining this way of understanding the Bible as Holy Scripture requires us to recognize the drama in its formation and contents.

Have you ever noticed how much our language assumes that we all are caught up in a great story, one that has a plot and an anticipated outcome? We often hear people say that something was "meant to be." On the other hand is the saying "You reap what you sow," or, in its updated version, "What goes around comes around." Our everyday language expresses our assumption that there is a bigger picture and that someone greater than we are is overseeing human affairs. At the same time we assume our freedom to either do right and influence the world positively, or do wrong and influence it negatively. That combination is the stuff of drama; life is filled with it, and so is the Bible. In the Bible we see that God relates to humanity as author of the drama.

I believe that the biblical account of the meaning of history anchors us at the Incarnation of God the Eternally Begotten.[4] The Grand Narrative reaches its climax in Jesus of Nazareth, in whom God has joined the drama that God authored and is authoring. Jesus Christ is the key to understanding history, and since the Bible is the primary source of our knowledge of Jesus Christ, the Incarnate Word, it is through the Bible that we learn God's intentions for history. The Bible itself is not the Incarnate Word; nevertheless, the Incarnation of God the Eternally Begotten epitomizes the way God is self-revealing. This is to say, the Incarnation is the complete expression of the pattern of God's self-revealing activity.[5]

Summary

This book is in large measure about the meanings and significance of the interrelated words that help us to express our beliefs about the Bible.

The number of "books" of the Bible is mostly, but not precisely, consistent among the major Christian traditions. The larger common core that all have in common is found in Protestant Bibles.

‹The Bible is the primary source for the truth and wisdom that guides Christian life and thought. It is our primary source because we believe God shepherded its formation; hence, we call it "Holy Scripture." ‹We bring our traditions, as well as reason and experience, to our interpretations.

Informed clarity of belief about the nature of the Bible and deliberately connecting our methods of interpretation to our beliefs is a matter of some urgency, given the challenges Christians are facing today, both within and outside the churches.

The way to understand the nature of the Bible that enables us to make the most sense of it as we turn to it for guidance is the one that best enables us to account for the dramas of life and history: that view is that the Bible's inspiration was incarnational in that it parallels the mysterious intersection of the divine and the human that was Jesus of Nazareth. It should not, however, be confused with Jesus the Incarnate Word, nor Jesus Christ with it.

In order to understand the Bible's inspiration and eventually to unpack an incarnational view of the Bible, we must first consider the theological concept of revelation. To that idea I turn in part one.

Questions for Discussion

◆ Describe any expectation you associate with reading or hearing the Bible. For example, do you expect God to speak to you or provide insight?

◆ How do your beliefs about God's involvement in the formation of the Bible influence your interpretations of passages that are crucial for addressing important ethical questions?

◆ What does the fact that Roman Catholic, Greek Orthodox, and Protestant Bibles have differences in their contents say about the Bible's reliability? Does the fact that the three great Christian traditions hold so many of the same ancient writings as sacred strengthen your confidence in the Bible?

◆ Do you think of the Bible as inerrant? Why or why not? Explain.

◆ Do you believe all interpretations of the Bible are equally valid? Why or why not? Explain.

Notes

1. The denomination I have in mind is my own, the American Baptist Churches in the USA.

2. Robert Funk, ed., *The Five Gospels: What Did Jesus Really Say? The Search for the Authentic Words of Jesus*, trans. Roy Hoover (New York: HarperCollins Publishers, 1997).

3. I am using these alternative terms out of sincere respect for my Jewish friends and neighbors.

4. I use this language instead of "God the Son," not because I object to the traditional language, but rather to avoid describing the eternal God as though God were male, and to suggest a less pronounced individuality in the Godhead.

5. The incarnational analogy for Scripture goes back at least as far as Origen of Alexandria; see Lewis Ayers, "Patristic and Medieval Theologies of Scripture: An Introduction," in *Christian Theologies of Scripture*, ed. Justin Holcomb (New York: New York University Press, 2006), 18. Recent books that explore this analogy as it may be applied to God's inspiration of Scripture include: Jeanine K. Brown, *Scripture as Communication: Introducing Biblical Hermeneutics* (Grand Rapids: Baker Academic, 2007); Peter Enns, *Inspiration and Incarnation: Evangelicals and the Problem of the Old Testament* (Baker Academic, 2005); most recently, Manfred T. Brauch, *Abusing Scripture: The Consequences of Misreading the Bible* (Downers Grove, Ill.: InterVarsity Press Academic, 2009).

Part I

Revelation

Case Study: Clash at a Pastors' Conference

A pastor was attending a conference. The participants, all pastors, were divided into three groups. The pastor's group learned meditative techniques to become centered during prayer. Conversations gravitated toward getting in touch with feelings and helping one another sort out those feelings.

Halfway through the week, the pastor challenged the leader about the goal of the prayer life he was recommending. The pastor suggested that Christian and Buddhist meditation have different goals. Buddhists seek tranquility; Christians seek peace. Did the group leader think there is a difference between tranquility and peace? He did not.

Later the same day, the leader described a moment in ministry when a parishioner had lost her spouse. The leader went to the widow's home. He told her he had no answers for her questions, no theological words of assurance. All he had to offer her was his presence: "I am here for you," he said.

In response to the leader's sharing, another member of the group asked a question that echoed the pastor's earlier concern: "What makes Christianity different from other religions?" Someone answered, "We have the Word of God." Another bristled, "But our interpretations are subjective!" Another asked, "Doesn't all human experience blend the objective and subjective dimensions of perception and understanding?" A short exchange followed. The conversation ended abruptly, without tranquility or peace.

Chapter One

Knowing About

"ALL INTERPRETATIONS are subjective!" "All is relative!" These declarations have influenced, in some cases permeated, many churches. The debate in our case study is often carried out with this vocabulary. The questions behind the debate ask if it is possible to know anything at all with confidence. And is it possible to know anything specifically about God and God's purposes for us? This latter is our first question.

At the heart of this debate are words and their meanings in general, and the meanings of several words in particular. Before moving on to several key terms, I will make three initial observations about words in general.

Of Words in General:
Forms, Histories, and Definitions

You may have noticed how teenagers use some of the same words you use, but with different meanings. They also create new words and new forms of old words in order to communicate with each other. The forms and meanings of a word may change over time. Here is an example from Church life of a word that changed both form and, to some extent, meaning as it passed from language to language and from generation to generation.

I am sure you are familiar with the word *bishop.* It came from ancient Greek, through French and early English, before arriving at its present form. (Greek and Latin provide the roots of many English words.) The ancient Greek word that *bishop* comes from has two parts, *epi,* meaning "over," and *scopein,* meaning, "to see." An *episcopos* was an "overseer." You may recognize the word *episcopos* in the English word *episcopal.*[1]

As words are used over long periods of time, vowels at their beginnings and endings that are peculiar to the grammar of the original language may fall away. *Episcopos* became something like *piscop*. Its hard consonants softened with use and *piscop* became *bisseop* and eventually *bishop*. Bishops, that is, overseers, lead episcopal churches. In early Christian circles, the one who was the overseer was the person who presided at Holy Communion, also called the Lord's Supper or the Eucharist. Justin Martyr, who was a second-century Church leader (often called a Church father), wrote that the bishop also oversaw the distribution of food to those who were in need.[2] Eventually, bishops acquired singular leadership authority over the churches in their city and its immediate geographical area.

Long usage is one way words develop more than one meaning. The differences among meanings sometimes are not readily apparent. Even so, a Methodist bishop is not the same in every way as a Lutheran bishop, nor is either of these the same in every way as a Roman Catholic bishop. What they have in common is the oversight of God's people in their churches. That is the core definition of the word *bishop*.

Guild Words

Think back to a time when you started a new job. You had to learn how words are used in that job or company. Most fields of employment use words that are unique to that profession, or use familiar words in unique ways: The idea of *filtering* means something different to a psychologist than it does to an engineer, and the word *belt* has a different meaning for a boxer than it does for a car mechanic.

You might think of each of the words I will be exploring as representing one thread in a tapestry. Please keep in mind that this tapestry, like all others, must be seen as a whole to be fully appreciated. Four key words are the primary threads in this tapestry: *revelation*, *inspiration*, *canon*, and *interpretation*. They are the titles of this book's four parts. "Incarnation" is the thread that runs through them all. For the moment, we will look to several other terms and ideas that are important, not only because they have often been used in relation to the word *revelation*, but also because they are part of the basic vocabulary of theological studies. Though you may not have heard these words, debates about them are at the center of a cluster of critical issues. The question before us in this chapter (about whether or not we can know the truth about God and God's purposes) engages an area of philosophy known as *epistemology*.

Epistemology

The Greek root of the word *epistemology* is *episteme*, which is translated into English as "knowledge."[3] Think of a scenic place where you love to go. What is in that place? How would you describe it to a friend? If your friend could see it with you, would your friend describe it as you would?

An exercise I use in one of my theology courses begins with an image of a meadow and three blossoming fruit trees. I ask the students how they determine what is in the scene. They say they use their sense of sight. Next I ask the class to identify the dominant color in the scene. It has a range of blended colors, so it is not easy to identify the dominant one. The class never agrees on the dominant color, but they do agree that there are three trees in the meadow. Based on our disagreement about the dominant color, they conclude that our perceptions involve more than the physics and physiology of sight. Perceptions result from sight *and* interpretation, and interpretation is at least in part subjective. If perceptions were not subjective, then every student would agree on the scene's dominant color and its other details. On the other hand, since they all agree that there is a picture and it contains trees in a meadow, our perceptions also must be at least in part objective. If they were not objective, then we could not honestly agree about any of the scene's components.

But what do I mean when I say our perceptions are objective and subjective? As I explain further my use of these words, keep in mind that, contrary to popular assumptions, knowledge gained by objective means is not necessarily true from every point of view, and subjective knowledge may be truer in its own way than objective facts. This, by the way, is why stories that draw out the meanings of events may be truer in their way than a factual outline of what happened.

Objective Knowing

Peter Angeles defines *objective* as: "[The] existence of an entity or an object in the external world (a) that is known, or (b) that can be known, and (c) that exists independently of our perception, conception, or judgment of it, as opposed to being merely a subjective existence in our mind or to being known in terms of our biases, feelings, and personal judgments."[4]

Think of a restaurant where you regularly eat. Let us say that I also dine regularly at the restaurant and I am sitting at the same table nearly every time you go there. So you have time to observe me (discreetly, of course). You know approximately how tall I am and whether I wear glasses, and so on. Over the course of several months you learn quite a lot about me. Up to this point you have objective knowledge of me. It is objective because it is acquired by observing from a "distance," by making someone or something the object of investigation.

Note that I put the word *distance* in quotes. I did this to signify that I mean something more than being across the room. The idea that knowledge may be gained objectively does not primarily refer to distance in time and space, though it may involve distance in this sense. The idea of objective knowledge also implies emotional distance. This is why we advise people whose emotions are raw after a difficult experience not to make any decisions that will have lasting consequences. We offer this advice because their emotions are "clouding their judgment," and so they are not "seeing things objectively." What we conclude based on observation is colored by our own prior experiences and present expectations. Our observations of the people we see are not purely objective. They always are subjectively informed as well.

Subjective Knowing

Continuing with our illustration we may say that if I, the object of your investigations, approach you and introduce myself, then you will have begun to know me personally. Perhaps by the glance of the eye or the firmness of the handshake you will now have perceptions and impressions that you could not have from a distance.

Conversation, especially when it is transparent, reveals more than "meets the eye." This kind of knowledge is subjective. According to Angeles, *subjective* may be defined as:

> referring to 1. that which is derived from the mind (the consciousness, the ego, the self, our perceptions, our personal judgments) and not from external, objective sources. 2. That which exists in consciousness but has no external, objective reference or possible confirmation. 3. That which is relative to the knower's own individual experiences (sensations, perceptions, personal reactions, history, idiosyncrasies).[5]

Subjective knowledge comes by relating to another, including through our more nuanced ways of communicating. This kind of knowledge is essentially relational. It cannot be acquired from a distance or by observation alone. Subjective knowledge of another person is acquired through interpersonal sharing. At its most subjective, it requires self-awareness, as it involves our feelings and intuitions. (We cannot communicate about ourselves if we are not self-aware!) Only mutual self-sharing enables us to say "We really connected" about another person, and once we have connected, that we know her. Rather than being the object of our curiosity, she has become a subject in communication, which is the basic ingredient of relationships.

John Baillie says interpersonal knowledge must be subject to subject; but, at the same time, he acknowledges that subject-to-subject communication is not entirely subjective. It has objective content without which the other person cannot be truly known. He goes on to say that it is not possible to know another person perfectly.[6] (Nor can we know ourselves perfectly.)

What I am claiming is that subjective knowledge, far from being necessarily inaccurate, adds to and may correct knowledge acquired by more objective means, especially of persons; but if our experience of subjective knowledge is to be comprehendible, if it is to be worthy of the word *knowledge*, then it also will have objective aspects. If I cannot describe another person's physical and emotional makeup, then I do not know that person well.

Back to Epistemology as Such

Now that I have explained basically the words *subjective* and *objective*, I can engage more directly the area of study called epistemology. At a very basic level, epistemology is about what we may know and how we are able to know it. In our day, most people in the Western world associate knowing with our senses. We saw the weakness of this in the class exercise above. As I said then, perception is more than seeing with our eyes. Scientists and philosophers remind us that what our senses report to our brains is interpreted by our minds. It is this interpretation that we see.

Influential German thinker Immanuel Kant probed the way the mind enables us to understand our world. He concluded that we can know anything only through our senses, but we know through our senses only as we fit into categories what our senses perceive.

Suppose you are seated at a table as you read this book. Your eyes and hands perceive the table and report their sensations to your brain — very different sensations of the same object. In order to know that what you are encountering is a table, you must put it into the table category. Once the sensory information is delivered in its various forms to the brain, the brain either fits that information into the category table that is already in the mind, or the brain expands or adds a category. If the table is a table like ones you have seen before, then you will identify it as a table. If it is in some ways unlike tables you have seen before, then you must expand the table category in your mind in order to perceive it as one. However, we cannot know anything in itself. What we perceive is itself an interpretation. Even with a common item like a table, the image in my mind when hearing the word *table* will inevitably be different in some way from yours because of our different prior experiences.

Since all the information we receive is filtered by the mind, we can know nothing directly, and certainly not as it is in itself. What we can know is only known according to our interpretation of what we see, hear, smell, taste, and touch, and this interpretation depends on the categories we already have or are able to establish in our minds. Even so, insofar as knowledge is verifiable, that knowledge comes to us through our senses.

According to Kant, this presents a serious challenge to the idea of knowing about God, since God cannot be observed with our senses. What we believe about God is not knowledge as such. God can only be the subject of faith.[7] This is because there is an extraordinary ontological difference between human beings and God. Ontology is our next important concept.

Ontology

The Greek root of the word *ontology* is *ontos*. It usually is translated "being." Hence, ontology may be defined as reasoning about kinds and ways of being.[8] An often used illustration of an ontological difference is to compare humans with so-called "lesser" animals. We will use dogs for our example.

If you have a dog, you know you have reasoning and creative abilities well beyond those the dog possesses. Dogs and humans are both animals and, more specifically, mammals. Despite this very basic similarity, the differences between dogs and humans are so wide and so many that biologists place us in different categories called *species*. This distinction seems justifiable as soon as we look at a person walking a dog (despite the similarities in appearance that sometimes are noted between masters and their canine companions).

In addition to looking very different than dogs, we humans, though smarter, do not have the keen senses that healthy dogs possess. We hear as humans do, not as dogs hear; we smell as humans are able to smell, not as dogs can. But we interpret what we see, touch, hear, and smell according to our ability to interpret, which is different from the same ability in dogs. In other words, as Kant said, humans may know only what our kind of being is able to know; dogs may know only what their kind of being is able to know. That is the ontological difference between us.

This difference is the reason communication between us and our dogs can be so very challenging. Simple words and gestures are the best we can do because humans, dogs, and other animals too may know only what our kind of being is able to know. And yet we are able to communicate on a rudimentary level. The greater animal trains the lesser to understand insofar as it is able, though sometimes we may wonder who is training whom. Communication happens!

This brings us back to our case of the meeting of pastors. Both sides in that disagreement were potentially right and both were potentially wrong. Communication happens among humans in person and in writing, and we can know the truth, but never perfectly. All perceptions are subjective; but not all that is subjective is untrue.

This does not, however, answer the question, Can communication happen between God and humans? The image of God in us notwithstanding (tarnished though it is), there is infinitely greater ontological distance between God and us than between us and dogs (forgive the comparison). Can we fallen humans know anything about God and God's purposes for us? The historic Christian answer to this question is yes, but humans need revelation from God about God and God's will, especially given our fallen condition.

Summary

In this chapter on knowing we have said that words represent ideas. The forms of words and the ideas or meanings they represent change over time.

The study of how we come to know what we know is called *epistemology*. Knowledge is acquired through subjective and objective means, and never exclusively the one or the other. Knowledge acquired by more objective means is not necessarily true from every point of view, and knowledge acquired by more subjective means is true in its own way.

Ontology is the study of ways and kinds of being or existence. God is ontologically very different from us. So much limits us! How can we possibly know about God, who transcends us absolutely? God must make God known.

Questions for Discussion

◆ How have you experienced the changing meanings of words and the challenges those changes bring to communication?

◆ How do you determine whether something is true? What standards and methods do you apply in order to make this determination?

◆ Is there a difference between truth and fact? How did you come to the answer you have given to this question?

◆ When you read the Bible, are you looking for truth or facts? Are you confident of the truth of your interpretations? Have you ever thought your interpretation of a passage was correct and another person's was incorrect? If yes, why?

Notes

1. *Oxford English Dictionary*, 1989, s.v. "Bishop."

2. Justin Martyr, "Apology," *Anti-Nicene Fathers*, vol. 1 (Peabody, Mass.: Hendrickson, 1985, 1994), 185.

3. "Epistemology" is "the theory of knowledge." *Oxford Dictionary of Philosophy*, ed. Simon Blackburn (Oxford: Oxford University Press, 1996), 123.

4. Peter Angeles, *The HarperCollins Dictionary of Philosophy*, 2nd ed. (New York: HarperCollins Publishers, 1992), 209. The philosopher Søren Kierkegaard based his work on the idea of subjective knowledge.

5. Ibid., 26.

6. John Baillie, *The Idea of Revelation in Recent Thought* (New York: Columbia University Press, 1956), lecture 2, 19–40.

7. Immanuel Kant has been criticized for dividing religious faith from real knowledge. For a very brief introduction to the ideas of Kant (and other philosophers), see Brian Magee, *The Story of Philosophy* (New York: Dorley Kindersley Publishing, 1998, 2001). An invaluable resource is Diogenes Allen's *Philosophy for Understanding Theology* (Philadelphia: John Knox, 1985).

8. "Ontology" is "a seventeenth-century coinage for the branch of metaphysics that concerns itself with what exists" (*Oxford Dictionary of Philosophy*), 267.

Chapter Two

Knowing in Person

WHEN YOU LOOK at the night sky and try to count the stars, is your imagination staggered by the immensity you see? When I look at the sky, I bump firmly against my inability to conceptualize infinity, let alone the eternal God! According to historic Christianity,[1] God is absolutely extraordinary when compared with us; so we say, God transcends us. You and I live in a particular time and place; but God is eternal and able to be everywhere. Since we are limited by so much, how can we possibly know about God, who transcends us so completely?

The historic Christian answer to this question is that God must make God known to us. This is what Christians refer to as "revelation." A second question suggested by our case study is, How is God self-revealing? God has come to us in person; God's self-disclosure was made full in Christ Jesus. The God of Isaiah's vision, who is "high and lofty," so "the hem of his robe filled the temple" (Isa. 6:1), is one with creation through the unique event of the Incarnation of the Word of God in Jesus Christ: "The Word became flesh and lived among us...full of grace and truth" (John 1:14). Other means of revelation are authoritative only as they are related to God's self-disclosure in the One whom the Gospel of John calls God's "Word."

Apart from this common core affirmation, Christians from various traditions do not listen to an identical range of persons, places, and writings for God's Word. When Roman Catholic Christians speak of revelation, they, officially at least, will mean the "tripod of truth." Alan Schreck, explaining this term, defines the tripod as "sacred Scripture, sacred tradition and the teaching office or Magisterium of the Church."[2] The Orthodox Churches recognize Scripture as "normative for the faith and life of the Church," but also stress "the role of the revelation of the living Word of God in . . . a dynamic revelation"[3] that happens between the Scriptures and the present life of the Church, especially as that is expressed in worship. Pentecostals, who are rightly suspicious of anything that may distance us from God, listen for God's immediate Word. They listen for God's Word in Scripture, in their own hearts and minds, and through one another.

So we may say that, according to the testimony of the wider body of Christ, God bears continuing living witness to God's nature and will through four sources. In addition to the Bible, there are tradition (especially as represented in worship and doctrinal statements), reason, and experience. These four, the so-called "Wesleyan quadrilateral," fit within the wider discussion of what I will call here the spheres of revelation.

The Two Spheres of Revelation

Think about hearing a sound or a voice and looking for where it was coming from. Sometimes the voice turns out to have originated very near you; it only sounds like it is far away. At other times, the voice may come from far away but seem to come from close at hand. It is the same with God's revelation. So we may ask, Is God's voice, so to speak, from far or near? A classic way of wording this is to ask, Is God's revelation from above or from below? Does God's word come to us from all around us or at particular times and from chosen individuals? These parallel another classic set of terms for describing God's revelation: *general revelation* and *special revelation.*

General Revelation

If you believe that knowledge of God comes only by a direct, highly particular, and intentional act of God, then you believe revelation comes from above and by special means. (Try not to associate above and below with up and down.) If you believe that God also may be known through what God has made, then you embrace revelation from below and in general.

Perhaps you have speculated about the traits of the person who made something you admired: "What are his or her habits, preferences, and the like?" In its most common form, the idea of general revelation is related to this experience. It is based on the belief that the entire creation reflects God; in much the way an artist's identity may be discerned by a close examination of a work of art. The psalmist recognized this: "The heavens declare the glory of God and the firmament proclaims [God's] handiwork." As the term suggests, general revelation occurs broadly, through creation (from below); it is indirect (we see what God has made and draw conclusions about God).

Suppose that we are neighbors, but we have never met. I have made a statue for my front yard. You notice the sculpture as you pass it daily. You talk about the sculpture at home. Based on what you see — colors, shapes, textures, theme — you draw conclusions about the sculptor. For reasons that are as much about you and the members of your household as they are about the statue, you decide that the sculptor must be a man, about fifty years old, short, rather religious, with no children. The motive for making the statue, you conclude, was to improve water flow in the yard.

Your conclusions, based on observations of what I have made, are only partly correct. I am a man. I am not very tall (even by my own estimation), I am in my fifties (I will be no more definite than that in writing), and I am religious (though I prefer to say that I love and strive to be faithful to Jesus of Nazareth, the Christ). However, you would be wrong about two very important details. I have one child, and my motive for making the statue was simply the love of creating.

This example demonstrates the ingredients of general revelation, or revelation from below. If you were my neighbor and if I had made a sculpture, then your knowledge of me would be derived from my creation rather than from direct encounter with me. Even if you were to touch and to smell the sculpture, your knowledge of me would remain indirect and impersonal, incomplete and not quite accurate in at least two very important ways.

If you believe God may be known from below and in general without the deliberate, immediate decision of God to use what is below for God's purposes, then you are assuming that one of two ideas is true: either God's "signature," so to speak, is on all that God has made, or God and creation are one.[4] (I prefer the former to the latter option.) On the other hand, if you believe God is known only by the deliberate, immediate decision of God to use what is below for God's purposes in revelation, then you believe revelation comes from above and God communicates through particular, special means.

Special Revelation

Many of us long for confidence that we can know God. After all, only God, who is the creator of all, knows the full meaning of our existence. We intuitively sense what further reflection confirms: left to ourselves, there is nothing we can know or say about the essential being of God. The only way to speak of God would then be in the negative, by way of what God is not. (Theologians use the Greek word *apophasis* for this, which means "denial.") According to the Christian faith, however, we are not left alone on an apophatic journey. While the psalmist and prophets knew God in personal ways, in Jesus Christ God came in person so we could know God in person. Based on this belief, Christians are able to know and to speak of God, however imperfect our speech and understanding may turn out to be. (Theologians use the Greek word *cataphasis* for this, which means "affirmation.")

Think about knowing someone close to you. I know my wife as I see her with my physical senses. I can describe her height, weight, and other features. This kind of knowledge is objective. Interpersonal knowledge is much more challenging to learn. There are some things about my wife that she must share if I am to know her in deeply personal ways. I can guess her mood based on past experience, but I cannot really know what she is feeling unless she tells me. Sometimes communicating with me about her thoughts and feelings is a real challenge, and not because she is not skilled at expressing herself!

If knowing someone personally is challenging for two human beings, it is no surprise that our efforts to understand God on our own are bound to lead at best to very limited results. After all, the ontological difference between God and us humans is infinitely great (especially since the Fall).

The belief that God is self-revealing in a personal way to specific individuals and communities is called "special revelation." A basic observation of those who emphasize knowing God exclusively through special revelation is that God can be known only as God communicates with us directly, deliberately, and personally.

Think again of the sculpture in my yard. If one day I see you stopping to look at my sculpture and I go outside to meet you, you will hear my voice and feel the touch of my hand when I introduce myself. If you linger long enough and I care to offer an explanation, you will hear directly from me about my sculpture. You will be able to ask me why I have made it and, in the course of our conversation, you will come to know me in person.

Another possibility is that I, the sculpture's maker, will not wait for you to knock on my door; I might take the initiative. If I want you to know the truth about me, I may write you a letter, or I may send my child to answer your questions. As I said earlier, special revelation is direct and communicated at particular times and places; it is personal, without necessarily being in person. But the more "in person" it is, the more confident we can be of God's character, intentions, and expectations.

This brings us back to objective and subjective knowing. I used the example earlier where you and I were in a restaurant. You might have come to very inaccurate conclusions about me by observation alone. You may have deduced that I am not married because I was not wearing a wedding ring. However, I may not wear a wedding ring due to religious preferences, even though I am, in fact, married. This is not to say that such observations from afar may not be the beginning of a deeper, more personal experience, but conclusions about God derived in this way are not necessarily true; indeed, they have been prone to error. "Objective gods are idols."[5] Special revelation, which is more fully interpersonal in its sharing and communicating, results in knowledge of a different order than is possible from below or through general revelation alone.

Embracing Above with Below
and Special with General

Most Christians intuitively embrace both of these perspectives. We rightly speak and think as if revelation comes both from above and from below, from special sources and in general. Here I will add that it proceeds from the transcendent through the immanent, to lengthen our list of contrasted terms. One of the places where we do this is through the hymns we sing.

What are your favorite hymns? Are they your favorites because of their melodies? Or do you like their lyrics too? Our churches' hymnals are sometimes called the "theology books of the Church." Contemporary and traditional hymns alike contain lyrics that celebrate the revelation of God.

The hymn "All Creatures of Our God and King," for example, invites all creation to praise God: "The flowers and fruits that in thee grow, let them God's glory also show!" (Ps. 19:1). As I write, it is fall in the northeastern United States. The colors are glorious. If nature is so splendid, then how much more so must be the God who created it! As nature "praises" God, it reveals something about God. In this case, nature reveals that God is glorious.

Hymns with lyrics about God's revelation frequently affirm the Bible. Amy Grant and Michael W. Smith's popular contemporary song "Thy Word" begins with biblical language: "Thy word is a lamp unto my feet, and a light unto my path" (Ps. 119:105, KJV). A favorite of mine, a more classic hymn, affirms the worth of God's Word: "How Firm a Foundation." I assume the composer is referring to the Bible. The hymn begins with the words of the title and then goes on:

> How firm a foundation ye saints of the Lord,
> is laid for your faith in His excellent word!
> What more can he say than to you he has said,
> to you who for refuge to Jesus have fled?

All together, these widely sung hymns express two sides of the Church's beliefs about the revelation of God to humanity. On the one hand they celebrate the evidence of God's worth in all of creation. (Let all creatures declare God's glory!) On the other hand they celebrate God's much more particular self-disclosures. (We can stand confidently on God's Word in times of struggle. It lights our paths on life's journey.) We see the intersection of these in Christ's own life and work, in the manner of God's inspiration of Scripture, and in the communities past and present that practice disciplined, prayerful interpretation of the Bible.

There are those who believe revelation must always be from above, or it is not really revelation. They deny any possibility that fallen human beings may know about God and God's purposes through nature and history. The Swiss theologian Karl Barth is famous for his determined opposition to the idea that anything about God may be learned through nature. For Barth revelation is always a deliberate, particular, and gracious act of God. There is just one ongoing act of revelation; it is initiated from above, but it occurs through Christ below. The transcendent God is personally present only through Christ and the Holy Spirit, about whom I shall have more to say in later chapters.

G. C. Berkouwer, another prominent theologian of the Reformation tradition, also believed that God's revelation really is just one work of God, not divisible into general and special expressions; but he believed that, in this fallen world, revelation has two manifestations. He says the terminology is weak, but there apparently is none better.[6] According to Berkouwer, we cannot know God sufficiently for salvation through general revelation alone. General revelation may lead us to the conclusion that we are guilty before the law of God and before the law of our consciences; but it is special revelation that teaches us about grace, and the means of it.[7] Indeed, it is through the special revelation of Jesus Christ that grace is offered to us.

The chapter's question was, How is God self-revealing? Our answer is, God speaks. Finally, as Karl Barth said, God's speech and action are one in the person of Jesus Christ. This is special revelation at its most focused — at its most particular. It is from above (special). Its source is the transcendent God; and yet God is self-revealing Godself through the immanence of human presence. The Incarnation of God the Eternally Begotten in Jesus of Nazareth is absolutely unique. In the Incarnation, revelation occurs from above through, and with the full participation of, what is below, not in general but in particular.

Summary

When we talk about divine revelation, we mean God's self-disclosure. Some say knowledge of God comes only by a direct, personal, and particular act of God. This is called special revelation, or revelation from above. Others say that knowledge of God may be discerned through what God has made, that God is revealed through all of creation. This is called general revelation, or revelation from below. Some believe God is self-revealing in both of these ways. But general revelation can lead by itself only to a sort of objective knowledge of God. The personal knowledge of God is revealed when God speaks. God's speech is God's act in Christ Jesus.

Questions for Discussion

- Think about your favorite hymns. Do you really believe what the words mean?

- Have you ever sensed God guiding you, giving direction through a sunset or a sunrise? From what sphere of revelation does that guidance come?

- Have you ever thought you sensed God guiding you while reading the Bible? Which are you more likely to follow, guidance through a sunset, or guidance through the Bible?

- How do you know your closest friend? Subjectively, objectively, or both?

- How does your Church help you to know God?

Notes

1. By *historic Christianity* I mean the beliefs that Christians throughout the ages of the Church have tended to believe at most times and places. See the works of Thomas C. Oden. One of his books where he discusses "paleo-orthodoxy" as the ground for historic ecumenical consensus is his *Systematic Theology*, vol. 1 (New York: HarperCollins, 1992), 321–74.

2. Alan Schreck, *The Essential Catholic Catechism: A Readable, Comprehensive Catechism* (Ann Arbor, Mich.: Charis/Servant Publications, 1999), 31.

3. Harold P. Scanlin, "The Old Testament Canon in the Orthodox Churches," in *New Perspectives in Historical Theology: Essays in Memory of John Meyendorff*, ed. Bradley Nassif (Grand Rapids: Eerdmans, 1996), 309.

4. Whether this may be called revelation as such is contested. Karl Barth is among those who have most vigorously challenged natural theology; see Karl Barth, *God in Action*, trans. Elmer G. Homrighausen and Karl J. Ernst (Manhasset, N.Y.: Round Table Press, 1963).

5. Statement added at the suggestion of Wesley Allen in a personal communication.

6. G. C. Berkouwer, "General and Special Revelation," in *Revelation and the Bible*, ed. Carl F. H. Henry (Grand Rapids: Baker Book House, 1958), 13–24.

7. Ibid., 19–22. Romans 1 suggests this about God revealed in nature.

Chapter Three

Knowing and Language

IN THE PREVIOUS CHAPTER, I made the point that we are able to know about God because God speaks. I also said that God's speech is God's action in Jesus Christ. Once again, Baillie states very succinctly the historic Christian point of view: "in [Christ Jesus] all revelation is comprehended and summed up."[1] Now there need be no doubting God's goodwill toward us because God came in person to make it plain. We might say "God walks the talk" with perfect integrity.

This affirmation raises other questions. The first is, What do we mean when we say God was Incarnate in Jesus the Christ? The second is, How can we experience special revelation today, since we are historically so far from Jesus Christ?

The Incarnation

The word *incarnation* comes from Latin. The prefix *in* was added to *carnatus*, which means flesh. Through the doctrine of the Incarnation we declare our belief that Jesus of Nazareth was God in the flesh. Christians have struggled from the beginning of the Church to understand how this could be.

The debate among early Christians had to do first with the relationship between Jesus of Nazareth and God. "Jesus is Lord!" was, arguably, the central affirmation of the apostolic churches. In saying this they identified Jesus Christ with God; and yet Jesus obviously was human. How could the man Jesus of Nazareth be God, and God be One God? The Incarnation seemed to threaten monotheism. After long and difficult debates, the first two great councils of the Church's bishops (Nicaea in 325 C.E. and Constantinople in 381 C.E.) declared that Jesus was fully

God ("of the same substance [*homoousios*] as the Father") and really human too ("was made flesh...was made human"). This formed the cornerstone of the doctrine of the Trinity.

Following this affirmation, conflict about how Jesus could have been both human and divine took center stage. Since divinity and humanity are so ontologically different, how could the two be mixed? To the Greek mind, God was perfect, eternal, and unchanging; but humans are subject to change and corruption. To the Jewish mind, God was (and is) Holy; but all humans sin.

A combination of important concerns drove the conversation about Jesus Christ. One was the need to understand who Jesus was, even in the face of what finally must remain a mystery. Another was the desire to be true to the Scriptures, and still a third concern had to do with the connection between Christ's person and Christ's work: who he was and what he came to do. Early Christian leaders believed that our understanding of Christ's ontological identity — his "personhood" — must correlate with our understanding of what Christ came to do for us. They recognized that what we believe about the one doctrine necessarily influences what we believe about the other.

Early Christian leaders believed, on the one hand, that only God could save fallen humanity. On the other hand, they believed that a human had to save us. They believed that if God had not taken on full humanity in Christ, Christ could not have cleansed humanity. They believed this because their basic principle for understanding how Christ saves was that "what has not been assumed cannot be restored; it is what is united with God that is saved."[2] Putting these beliefs together, the humanity and the divinity of Jesus Christ must have been united in him. If they were not, then he could not have saved us. But the divine and the human also had to remain distinct in order to remain what they were. If the human and divine were so united in Christ as to be mixed with each other, then Christ could not have saved us, because the divine would not have remained truly God and Jesus would not have remained truly human in their union. If only God could save us and a human had to save us, then a hybrid Christ a "third thing" (Tertullian's *Tertium quid*), which would have been neither human nor divine, could not have saved us.

At the Council of Chalcedon (451 C.E.), the bishops of the churches decided that Christ's nature had to be divine and human at the same time: truly (Greek, *alethos*) God and truly (*alethos*) human. They concluded further that the divine and the human natures had to be united in the one person of Christ, and that Christ's humanity and divinity could not be confused in their unity.

The doctrine of the Incarnation was and is mind-bending to try to comprehend — no one can understand it fully. It seems especially illogical to the modern mind-set, as does so much ontological speculation about mysteries. Since there is no analogy for the Incarnation in human experience (even helpful illustrations are difficult to find),[3] many call it a contradiction and reject it; others call it paradoxical. I prefer to describe it as dialectical. Dialectical thinking helps us to see a kind of internal logic to the Incarnation. *Dialectic* is the next critical term for our study.

Thinking Dialectically

The word *dialectic*, like every word, has a history. It is related to our word *dialogue*. According to Peter Angeles, the ancient Greek philosopher Heraclitus employed it to refer to "the process of change in thought and the universe whereby all things pass over into what they are not, and were not (opposites)."[4] Perhaps you have sat on the edge of a stream and dipped your feet in the water. Heraclitus claimed that we could not step into the same river twice. The river is always changing. There is the river that was, and there is the river that is.

Plato also used the word *dialectic*, but more broadly. He used it of "the rational, philosophical method in general"[5] whereby truths are arrived at by placing seemingly contradictory ideas side by side in order to see what really can be known. And the meaning of the word has continued to develop since then.

I define *dialectic* as something more like a dialogue between two ideas that seem at first to be contradictory but turn out to be mutually and dialogically interdependent. This is different than understanding dialectic as relating ideas that are assumed to be (1) in perpetual opposition and are therefore either to be left alone; or (2) resolved into a synthesis that leaves neither idea fully what it is.[6] Instead of placing ideas in a position of "over-against-ness," I suggest that dialectic may be understood as a dialogical relationship between two apparently opposite but conceptually interdependent ideas. Each is fully intelligible individually only if the other is fully affirmed.

Here is a theological example. You may have wondered how it is that God can be both just and merciful. One of the great twentieth-century theologians, Reinhold Niebuhr, commented helpfully on the relationship between justice and mercy. If there were no justice there would be no need for mercy because there would be no basis for conviction; and yet without mercy justice would cease to be justice, as it would degenerate into vengeance.[7]

We see the resolution of the dialectical relationship between justice and mercy on the cross, where Christ Jesus fulfilled the demands of justice as he performed the ultimate act of mercy. Justice and mercy need each other in order to be fully what they are. This is a dialectical relationship.

Looking back again to the Incarnation, we may note that, in order for Christ to save, he had to be human, and yet God alone could save us; God alone could save us, and yet a human had to do it. Only as both divine *and* human could Jesus Christ be the One Savior. This too is a dialectical relationship.

I said above that there is no analogy for the Incarnation, but now I will qualify that statement. There is one possible analogy for it: language. It is no accident that Jesus was called the Word of God (John 1:1–18).

Our Dependence on Words

Our second question in this chapter is: How can we experience special revelation today, since we are historically so far from Jesus Christ the Word of God Incarnate? The historic Christian answer is that it is through the Bible and tradition — through words — that we learn most authoritatively about Christ Jesus. The more precise answer for Protestants is that we learn authoritatively about Jesus Christ through the Bible most of all. But we are not, after all, merely people of the Book; we are people in Jesus Christ. Nevertheless, we are word-dependent. We need the Bible for detailed and confident knowledge of Christ, his person and work; of God and God's will.

Language: Objective and Subjective

Alan Schreck, the Roman Catholic theologian whom I quoted in chapter 2, says this about revelation:

> Even when that which we think or say about God is true, our words cannot adequately express his perfection or simplicity. The best human concepts and images are more *unlike* God than like him. Nonetheless, this should not deter us. We rejoice in the glimpse of God and his presence that we find in his creation, in what we term "natural revelation." Even when God chooses to reveal himself more directly, in what we call "divine revelation" [what we are calling here "special revelation"] *he still presents himself within the limits of human perception and understanding.*[8]

Language provides the framework for our perceptions and understanding of the world. It epitomizes[9] our experience of the blending of the objective and subjective dimensions of reality, of revelation from above and from below, special and general, and, I will add here, of meaning and form. As powerful as language is as a means of communication, it is limited; as limited as language is, it remains a powerful (our best) tool for communication.

Pause for a moment. Close your eyes and see what is in your mind. Is there dialogue going on between and among your thoughts? That dialogue can be hard to quiet; I know it is for me. You may have noticed that you visualize much of what you are saying to yourself. Our understanding is organized according to progressions of ideas represented by words.

Words are symbols of a kind. On a very basic level, they are pictures of the ideas they represent. Just as word-symbols are made up of combinations of the individual symbols we call letters, sentences are symbols resulting from combinations of the symbols we call words.[10] In order for ideas to be communicated, they must conform to an order that both the speaker and the listener recognize.

We can see more readily that words are symbols when we see writing in a language that uses a different alphabet than ours. For example, the Greek word for house is οικος. The symbol οικος stands for a house. If you memorize this symbol in connection with its meaning, you will think of a house whenever you see it. English is written with Latin letters (symbols). Each letter represents a sound. When letters are put together to form a word, they all together become a single, more complex symbol associated with combinations of sounds and meanings, to sentences and paragraphs, and so on.

Like all symbols, words have meaning. More precisely, they have definitions, which is to say they mean something in particular; otherwise, we could not discuss houses or tables or other things we have been discussing in this book. The definitions of words are the ideas they represent. It is in light of the definitions and common uses of words that I am deciding as I write this book what I believe are just the right words for what I want to say. So, I say words are objective. If words were not objective, they would have no definitions and we would not understand each other when we speak.

However, words also are subjective. The picture in your mind that you associate with the word *house* may be very different from the picture that enters my mind. I am thinking of the house I now reside in; you may be thinking of the house where you grew up. Both images will fit the category to which we attach the word *house*, but if words were only objective, there would be no accounting for the varieties of interpretations there may be of a single word or phrase. Said another way, if words were perfectly objective, there would be no miscommunication; if they were only subjective, there would be no communication. Words have definitions, but usually those definitions are not perfectly clear.

The dialectic of meaning and words is like that between the divine and the human in Christ. Meaning is not the same as a word; a word is not the same as its meaning; neither are meanings and words separable from each other. They are united through the intention of the one who uses them. (This paragraph is so important that you should read it at least twice!)

Completing the Circle[11]

Have you ever felt as though the person to whom you are speaking was not paying attention to what you were saying? I imagine all of us have experienced this. At times — too often, I fear — I have been the distracted culprit in miscommunication.

The more profound or personal we think what we are saying is, the more we want the person listening to be attentive. When we ask, "Are you really listening to me?" our hope is that the answer will be "Yes." "Revelation" from one person to another requires a response. Unless we have heard the person speaking and received what the person says so as to respond in a way that connects with the speaker, revelation is incomplete; the circle is broken. The speaker's words have "fallen on deaf ears," as we say.

It is very satisfying, on the other hand, to receive a response that demonstrates that we have been heard, that the other person has "decoded" the meaning of our word symbols correctly and has heard in a way that honors what we have said.

When we believe we are in the presence of an authority, we are more likely to listen attentively. How much more should this be the case when we trust that — have faith that — God is inspiring the speaker! Revelation demands a response. According to John Baillie the required response to God's revelation is faith. Faith may be understood in more than one way. Faith is assent; faith is commitment; faith is trust. For Baillie and those he cites, faith as trust is primary.[12] When we trust the person to whom we are listening, we hear that person differently than we would if we did not trust him or her, because in the act of trusting, we assent to the one who is trusted and commit to the relationship in which trust is the appropriate response.

The Effect of Reception

The purpose of revelation is not fulfilled until revelation is received in faith. Once received in faith, our interpretation may be different than it otherwise would have been.

Think back to the illustration I shared about knowing my wife. I said she must share some things about herself if I am really to know her. She communicates with me through words and actions. For example, she may wash my clothes at a time when she knows I am very busy. Through that action she may be communicating her love and care for me. What enables me to come to that conclusion is the trust built on many years of experience. When we know a person well, we have important additional information that helps us to interpret the person's actions. My past experience with my wife leads me to conclude reflexively that she intended to communicate love and care by washing my clothes. She is not the type who would try to make me feel guilty for not doing my wash in a timely fashion. Experience influences our interpretations; more precisely, experience has taught me to trust Jana, and I interpret her actions in that light.

Even though I trust Jana, the way to know her intention with confidence is to ask her. Yet even verbal language may be misinterpreted, not only when spoken but also when written. The meanings of words depend very much on when, how, and why they are used. Just as there is a dialectical relationship between meaning and words, there is one between contexts and meanings. (I will say more about this later.) Faith makes all the difference in our ability to receive God's Word through the Bible.

The Bible as Revelation

We are not alone in interpretation as we trust the Holy Spirit, working in and through the community of the faithful, to speak to us through the words of Scripture. According to the biblical testimony to Jesus' teaching, God sent the Holy Spirit to lead us "into all truth" (John 16:13). Yes, we are dependent on the prophetic and apostolic interpretation of the historic events to which they bear witness. Yes, they convey their testimony through language, and we receive their testimony in our own very different times and places (contexts). But Christians historically have believed that the Holy Spirit of God, the third Persona of the Trinity (*Persona* suggests personal distinction without implying individual human persons),[13] shepherds the community of Christ to interpret the apostolic witnesses. Shepherds guide their sheep; they do not choose each step the sheep take. As the Spirit shepherded the writers and editors of the Bible, the Spirit stirs a response in us when we read or hear it.

This stirring is what we call inspiration, and it is to the idea and experience of inspiration that we will turn in part 2.[14]

Summary

According to Christian belief, special revelation finally was so specific to time and place as to be completely personal in Christ Jesus. The doctrine of the Incarnation is the historic Christian understanding of the person of Jesus Christ. Early Christians understood Christ's person in light of his work; specifically, what he accomplished for us.

Dialectical thinking helps us to understand key theological ideas. Dialectic may be understood as a dialogical relationship between two apparently opposite but conceptually interrelated ideas or affirmations that turn out to be mutually dependent.

It is no accident that the Eternally Begotten One is called God's Word. Words, verbal language, epitomize our experience of the blending of the objective and subjective dimensions of reality. Relational knowing, as it is both objective and subjective, is a dialectical, linguistic experience: "The Word became flesh...we have seen his glory, the glory as of a father's only son, full of grace and truth." (John 1:14)

Through the Bible, the Holy Spirit bears witness to Christ. The Spirit bears witness in our hearts to the truth of apostolic testimony — testimony to what God did, and to what God is doing.

Given the fact that language is dynamic, so integrative of objective and subjective dimensions of knowing, how can writers bear, and readers and hearers receive, this witness?

This brings us to the subject of the inspiration of the Holy Spirit.

Questions for Discussion

♦ Why is it difficult to communicate with others, even when they are seated next to us and have had similar experiences?

♦ Why is it difficult to say anything about God with absolute confidence?

♦ How is it possible to communicate with others, even when they are not seated next to us and their experiences are very different from ours?

♦ How is it possible to say anything with confidence about God?

♦ Why are words not enough for us to understand God's character and will for us? On the other hand, why are they sufficient?

♦ Have you found dialectical thinking to be helpful for your faith?

Further Reading

Barth, Karl. *God in Action*. Trans. Elmer G. Homrighausen and Karl J. Ernst. Manhasset, N.Y.: Round Table Press, 1963.

Bloesch, Donald. *Holy Scripture: Revelation, Inspiration and Interpretation*. Downers Grove, Ill.: InterVarsity Press, 1993.

Boone, Kathleen. *The Bible Tells Them So: The Discourse of Protestant Fundamentalism*. London: SCM, 1990.

Holcomb, Justin S., ed. *Christian Theologies of Scripture: A Comparative Tradition*. New York: New York University Press, 2006.

Morrison, John Douglas. *Has God Said? Scripture, The Word of God, and the Crisis of Theological Authority*. Evangelical Theological Monograph Series 5. Eugene, Ore.: Pickwick Publications, 2006.

Webster, John. *Holy Scripture: A Dogmatic Sketch*. Cambridge: Cambridge University Press, 2003.

Notes

1. John Baillie, *The Idea of Revelation in Recent Thought* (New York: Columbia University Press, 1956), 80.

2. This idea is associated with Gregory Nazianzen and Gregory of Nyssa. The divine had to take on every aspect of humanity in order for the whole of us to receive the work of Christ on our behalf; see J. N. D. Kelly, *Early Christian Doctrines*, rev. ed. (San Francisco: HarperSanFrancisco, 1960, 1978), 297.

3. An analogy (from Greek *ana* + *logos*, to say something again) has in itself something of what it points to; an illustration just parallels what it points to.

4. Peter A. Angeles, *The HarperCollins Dictionary of Philosophy*, 2nd ed. (New York: HarperPerennial, 1992), 71–72.

5. Ibid., 71.

6. The first is Kant; the second is Hegel.

7. See, for example, Reinhold Niebuhr's sermons and prayers, collected by Ursula Niebuhr in *Justice and Mercy* (New York: Harper and Row, 1974).

8. Alan Schreck, *The Essential Catholic Catechism: A Readable, Comprehensive Catechism* (Ann Arbor, Mich.: Charis/Servant Publications, 1999), 13 (emphasis mine).

9. *Epitome:* "something that forms a condensed record or representation 'in miniature,'" def. 2, *Oxford English Dictionary*, 1933, s.v. "Epitome."

10. St. Augustine of Hippo wrote about language as sign in his work "On Christian Doctrine," book 2, *Nicene and Post-Nicene Fathers*, series 1, vol. 2 (Peabody, Mass.: Hendrickson Publishers, 1887, 1994), 535–55.

11. The "hermeneutical circle" is more involved than what I am discussing in this section. For brief descriptions, see Kent Sparks, *God's Word in Human Words* (Grand Rapids: Baker Academic, 2008), 38; Garrett Green cites Werner Jeanrond in *Theological Hermeneutics and Imagination: The Crisis of Interpretation at the End of Modernity* (Cambridge: Cambridge University Press, 2000), 7.

12. Baillie, *The Idea of Revelation in Recent Thought*, 83–108.

13. The early Christian theologian Tertullian, who was from North Africa, invented this phrase to describe the Trinity: *una substantia, tres personae* (one substance, three persons).

14. Sometimes a distinction is made between inspiration of the biblical text and the illumination of the reader. I see the work of the Holy Spirit in conveying God's Word as one work from beginning to end, and prefer the word *inspiration* because the term has *spir* at its root, which better accommodates the local specificity of special revelation.

Part II

Inspiration

Case Study: God Is Everywhere

A young man, Dave, is studying theology. While in search of a new Church home, he begins attending Christian Church Anywhere.

The lay leader of this Church oversees its ministry of hospitality and tries to get acquainted with Dave during a coffee hour. Early in the conversation, Dave describes his enthusiasm for the study of theology. Since the lay leader shares this interest, the conversation takes off. Dave's intellectual life is well cultivated, but his spiritual life is harder to get a handle on.

"Is there a place where you go to pray?" the lay leader asks. Dave answers by describing walks in the woods where he senses God's presence. He goes to the woods because he believes God is in all things. Connecting with God in a setting that is serene, quiet, and filled with life enables him to hear God within.

"Do you ever study the Bible?" the lay leader asks. Dave says he does.

"Do you hear God through the Bible the way you hear God in the woods?"

Dave answers, "I do. But I also hear God in other great books. I believe the Bible is inspired, but I do not believe it is more inspired than other great works of literature."

The people responsible for cleaning up after coffee hour signal that it is time to vacuum the floor. Dave has to get back to his studies; the lay leader is scheduled to accompany the pastor on visits to the homebound.

Chapter Four

Stirred Up

THE UNIVERSITY STUDENT looking for a Church home embraces a panentheistic (God is in everything) understanding of God's presence in the world.[1] How is this belief informing his experience of inspiration? How are his feelings when he is in the woods influencing his understanding of God's way of communicating with us? How is biblical inspiration like and unlike his experiences in the woods?

As we continue to weave, thread by thread, the tapestry of an incarnational understanding of the nature of the Bible and to link that theology with the way we interpret it, we must clarify what inspiration is and explore how the general way of describing the experience of inspiration compares with four ways of understanding the inspiration of the Bible (in chapter 6).

Inspiration in General

I am sure you have had the experience of being deeply moved, intellectually and emotionally, by someone or something. You may have heard music that thrilled you and permanently changed your taste in music; or you may have read a book that challenged you to see life differently than you saw it before. You may have seen a movie that "warmed your heart" and got you to thinking differently than before; or you may have witnessed an act of self-sacrifice that demonstrated love so well that you have not behaved quite the same way since.

I was inspired the first time I heard (really heard) classical music. My mother had given me a set of record albums for my twelfth birthday. They contained selected passages from the most popular compositions of many classical composers. I never will forget how I felt the first time I listened to them. One piece was particularly memorable. My spirit soared at the sound of the broad, swift, and dramatic musical phrases of Felix Mendelssohn's "Italian Symphony." I have appreciated classical music ever since then. It calms or energizes me, as the music and the occasion require.

The stirring that is inspiration is not just emotional. It is an experience of inward integration; or put another way, inspiration brings mind and heart together in a moment of clarity that resonates deep within, and changes us.

Of course, this is a very basic definition. Like the other words we have explored, the word *inspiration* has a history. The English word *inspiration* is from the Latin *inspiratus*. You may recognize the root of in*spir*ation in another English word, re*spir*atory, which has to do with breathing. In human medicine, a rate of respiration is the number of breaths a person takes in a given period of time. The images of breath and breathing are very much at the root of the definition of inspiration.

There are two Latin verbs related to the noun *inspiratus*: one is *inspirare* and the other is *inspiratio*. The first verb has more to do with breathing air into something or someone, as when a person administering CPR breathes into the person in need of reviving. The second has more to do with drawing air into oneself, as when a person emerging from underwater takes a deep breath to fill the lungs to capacity. The English definitions of inspiration reflect these varieties in the Latin.[2]

The first definition offered in Webster's Dictionary is theological. It is attached to the verb *inspirare*. Inspiration is "a divine influence or action upon the lives of certain persons that is believed to qualify them to receive and to communicate sacred revelation and is interpreted within Christianity as a direct action of the Holy Spirit."[3] Notice that this definition is objective in the sense that the source of inspiration is outside of the person being inspired; it is subjective in that it refers to the experiences and subsequent qualities of persons receiving that divine action.

The lay leader in our case study may have this understanding of inspiration. She is concerned that David's listening for God in the woods is too subjective, so she wants to know if David consults the Bible, which she apparently believes offers more definitive guidance from God. She does not deny the value of his experience with God in the woods, but she wants him to have a relationship with God, the true God. You will recall that knowing another person (relational knowing) blends both objective and subjective ways of knowing.

The second definition in Webster's Dictionary emphasizes the subjective side of the experience of inspiration. It arises from *inspiratio,* and refers to "the act of breathing in," or, more specifically, "the drawing of air into the lungs — as opposed to expiration."[4] Where the first definition balances outside influence and its effect on the person receiving it, the second leans toward the subjective, since it emphasizes the person receiving and experiencing the inspiration.

The lay leader in our case study is insightful. Even though Dave is listening for God, whom he believes is outside of him in nature, he does not listen for God through what is outside of him. Dave believes God also is within him; and that is where, he believes, God's voice must be heard. It is Dave's experience that God's voice within us is best heard in the context of the woods, where life is so abundant, and, according to Dave, God's Spirit dwells in a sort of concentrated way. The lay leader suspects that Dave's expectations, coupled with the serenity of the setting, merely allow his own thoughts, emotions, and intuitions to come to the surface, and that it is not necessarily God whom Dave is hearing from within.

The third definition leans toward the objective aspects of inspiration. According to Webster's, it is "the act or power of moving the intellect or emotions: capacity to inspire." The dictionary gives an example: "the inspiration of this lovely scene."[5] The scene is a place; that is an objective fact. Of course, there is a subjective element here too. The inspiration of the scene is merely potential until there is a subject to receive it. You, or I, or Dave.

It seems that the concern of the lay leader is that Dave is not being challenged to grow in the direction God would have him grow. This is because there is no inspired corrective for his own private preferences and impulses; the lay leader believes that without the Bible, Dave is not really in touch with the fuller guidance God may provide. No doubt the lay leader is relieved when Dave says he listens for God speaking in the

Bible too; but he does not listen to the Bible as a necessarily convincing or convicting authority. Other books also are inspired and inspiring for Dave, and he grants them equal status with the Hebrew and Christian Scriptures.

The lay leader recognizes that when we face ethical decisions, as in the controversial issues I raised in part 1 (abortions, women in professional ministry, etc.), we need more than sentiment or intuition to guide us. When faced with ethical dilemmas, we want and need a more definitive word than Dave likely receives through his inner voice. Careful, informed thinking is necessary for addressing complex ethical issues. People whose ethics are derived from careful thinking about the life and ministry of Jesus, which we know principally from the Gospels, hear a more specific and more compelling Word than nature or the inner human self alone can speak. We need a word from above that speaks compellingly to our particular situation. While nature may inspire thoughts and feelings about God, it is in the person of Jesus the Christ that God introduced us to God and taught us God's purposes for us. T. F. Torrance said this very well: "[I]t was by the eternal Son or Word of God who became man in Jesus Christ that God the Father Almighty was the Maker of heaven and earth and of all things visible and invisible."[6] It is through the biblical witness to Jesus Christ that we know this: it is in *The Book*.

The Unique Case of Books

Paintings, like pictures, are "worth a thousand words," as the saying goes. While we are able to interpret a painting in ways that are meaningful for us without talking with the painter, it is by getting in touch with the master who painted the painting that we may know with confidence what the painter really meant to communicate through his or her work. For most of us, painters are seldom if ever available in person to the average appreciator of their art. Similarly, composers are seldom if ever available in person to their listeners.

Obviously, books are a different kind of medium for communication than paintings or music. Careful authors select just the right words, just as painters select just the right colors and shapes, and composers just the right notes and tempos; but words are a more definitive means of communicating. Careful authors select "just the right words" to say what they want to say (perhaps not so aptly as we or the author might like). Books may stimulate the imaginations of their readers. But as masterful as great authors are, they do not control our imaginations; nor can we see into theirs. Despite the strength of language for communicating more precisely, language also leaves room — sometimes a great deal of room — for interpretation. However, books have just the configurations of words that are in them and those words limit the range of meanings that may be derived from them.

Authors, Texts, and Contexts

When we interpret a text, questions may arise that lead us to wish the author were available for additional conversation. Access to the author through the author's written words is never complete, for several reasons: the breadth and depth of language's meaning, the dependence of inspiration and communication on common ground in language and thought forms, varying contexts between authors and readers, all complicate communication, especially in writing.

A class exercise I use helps students feel one difference between the spoken word and the written word. I ask them to think of a belief of theirs that seems unusual. I ask them to share that belief in confidence with the person sitting next to them. Then I ask them to write down that belief. At that moment, not yet knowing what I plan to do with what they may write, some students are tempted to alter what they said to their classroom neighbor.

Why are we more careful with what we write than with what we speak? We are more careful with what we write because words have a life of their own, especially as they move beyond the author's availability to clarify what she or he meant to say. We have some anxiety about having our words taken out of context. The meaning we get out of our reading and that others get out of our writing, may be more — much more — than the meaning the author intended to convey. Texts have a life of their own, especially apart from their author and their author's context.

Here is an example. You may have read C. S. Lewis's classic series of children's books called *The Chronicles of Narnia*. The second and third volumes of the seven were produced as movies. If you saw them, you may agree with me when I say the movie versions of the stories were very well done; but they do not tell the stories exactly as Lewis wrote them. As soon as Lewis published them, the stories took on a life of their own.

The way a text inspires us depends on our life-experiences and settings. For meaning to be communicated there must be common ground in language and experience between the author and the reader. There are subtleties in Lewis's book that you and I may miss. Though I speak English and live in an English-speaking culture, my efforts to interpret Lewis are complicated by the fact that he wrote from within the culture of Great Britain in the mid-twentieth century. I live in the United States in the early twenty-first century. *The Lion, the Witch and the Wardrobe* inspires me, but it would not necessarily inspire everyone who reads the book or sees the movie, and certainly not everyone in the same way. It may not inspire us quite the way Lewis intended.

There is room for interpretation and confusion for many reasons. As I wrote above: the breadth and depth of language's meaning, the dependence of inspiration and communication on common ground in language and thought forms, varying contexts between authors and readers, all complicate communication, especially in writing. These complications do not, however, inhibit completely an author's effort to communicate ideas, nor our effort to understand them. The fact that they are not insurmountable is evident in the fact that meaning can be shared across cultural distances. *The Chronicles of Narnia* are a case in point. Lewis wrote *The Chronicles* in a way that inspires many, and that from his context to theirs; so, I say, Lewis has expressed transcultural truths through the culturally conditioned forms Lewis used to freight his meaning. The meaning some readers find in these stories is not always the meaning Lewis intended; but such interpretations are not therefore in error. It seems to me that the word *error* applies when interpretations are actually contrary to an author's intention, as discerned through the language expressed.

While I appreciate the fact that language as bearer of meaning is necessarily contextual, I am persuaded that meaning transcends the confines of particular languages.[7]

Back to Inspiration

Books provide a more definitive word — *message* — than other forms of "mass" communication; so we Christians look to our Book when we are asking how best to live. The inspiration that comes from books raises questions about the intentions of authors, the status of texts, and the life setting of the readers compared with those of the authors. If reading a book inspires you, must the author also be inspired? Can a book be inspired in and of itself, apart from the author's intention or genius? If a book inspires some but not others, then is the inspiration really in the person reading it?

The way we speak about inspiration reflects the imprecision of our answers to these questions. We may say of a writer that "she is inspired," or we may say "that book is inspired." We also may say, "He inspired me; or, I was inspired by her." There are other, related questions; like, Whose meaning is decisive? And is it legitimate to derive a meaning from a text that an author may not have intended? These questions fall within the area of study and thinking called "hermeneutics" (especially its philosophical form), which I will define in the next chapter.

Back to Our Question

How is biblical inspiration the same as and different from inspiration in general? Historically, Christians have believed that it was God who inspired the composition and formation of the Bible. That is the essence of the difference, but the actual experience of God's inspiration may have been more like a still small voice than a thunderous earthquake. I think it would have had the same blending of personal objective/subjective encounter about it that we see in other experiences of personal inspiration. If the inspiration of the biblical authors and editors was out of the ordinary, then I believe it was something more like people's experience with Christ's revelation of himself to the two disciples on the road to Emmaus: "Were not our hearts burning within us when he spoke to us on the road, while he was opening the Scriptures to us?" (Luke 24:32). They were deeply stirred; but they didn't recognize it at first.

This leads to our next question: What does the Bible say about its own inspiration? Among Christians, there is not just one answer to this question.

Summary

I set out in this chapter to explore what it means to say someone or something is inspired or inspiring. This required talking about inspiration in general and distinguishing inspiration in general — of painters and composers and of us looking at nature — from the inspiration of the Bible.

In this chapter I have said that "inspiration is an integrating inward experience that brings mind and heart together in a moment of clarity that resonates deep within us and changes us." I have said that the English definitions found in a dictionary demonstrate that inspiration has objective and subjective aspects (never just one or the other). Some people emphasize the objective aspects of it, while others focus on its subjective dimensions. I have said that ethical decisions require careful reasoning, and, for theists, a more definitive word from God if they are to be arguably more than just the intuitions of individuals and communities. Authors are able to communicate through books more definitively than composers and painters are able to do through their arts. Nevertheless, as powerful a tool as language is, varying contexts and the range of meanings that may be ascribed to what is written render language a more challenging medium of communication than many think it is.

Questions for Discussion

◆ When have you been inspired? Was it through a song, a book, a scene from nature?

◆ When you are inspired, do you assume God is in that inspiration? Why? When?

◆ When you are about to read the Bible, do you seek something different than you do when you are about to begin a novel? A book of science? A book of history? Why?

◆ When you are facing ethical dilemmas, where do you go for guidance? Why?

Notes

1. Sallie McFague advocates panentheism, to be distinguished from pantheism, in *Models of God: Theology for an Ecological, Nuclear Age* (Minneapolis: Augsburg Fortress Press, 1987). *Pan* is the Greek prefix meaning all or every; *theos* is the Greek word meaning God. Pantheism is the belief that God is all things, and all things are, therefore, divine. The Greek prefix *en* means "in." So *pan* + *en* + *theos* means God in all things. Panentheistic theology is an adjusted form of process thought.

2. *Webster's Third New International Dictionary of the English Language,* 1965, s.v. "Inspiration." David R. Law has written an excellent study of inspiration: *Inspiration* (New York: Continuum, 2001).

3. *Webster's Third New International Dictionary.*

4. Ibid.

5. Ibid.

6. T. F. Torrance, *The Trinitarian Faith: The Evangelical Theology of the Ancient Catholic Church* (London: T. & T. Clark, 2000), 89.

7. For more on speech-act theory and authorial intention, see Kevin Vanhoozer, *Is There a Meaning in This Text? The Bible, the Reader, and the Morality of Literary Knowledge* (Grand Rapids: Zondervan, 1998.)

Chapter Five

Stirred by Whom?

DO YOU APPROACH reading the Bible expecting to hear from God? Do you pick it up with reverence? Does the thought of reading it stir your heart with warm affection for the wisdom and guidance you glean from it? With warmth for God? Most Christians I have known treat the Bible with respect. Why? We believe God had a hand in forming it, and God meets us "through its pages."

In the last chapter, I discussed the word *inspiration* as it is used in regard to movies, literature, and such. Now I must turn our attention to the question, What does it mean to say the Bible is inspired by God? The question of God's inspiration of the Bible often leads those already inclined toward Christian faith to ask what the Bible "says" about its own inspiration.

I wrote in part 1 that controversies surrounding the issues that are straining the unity of many churches and denominations often hinge on differing beliefs about the nature of the Bible and how it may be rightly interpreted. It does not take long in the course of such discussions for the idea of "inspiration" to take center stage. An often-quoted verse is 2 Timothy 3:16, "All Scripture is inspired by God and is useful for teaching, for reproof, for correction, and for training in righteousness." At the heart of this verse is the idea of "inspiration," and not merely inspiration in general, but of the Bible in particular. If you have been involved in discussions of this verse, then you are aware that those who champion the cause of the divine authorship of the Bible believe this verse demonstrates that the Bible "claims" to be inspired by God.

In order to assess the impact of this and related passages on our question, we must deal eventually with the theory and methods of biblical interpretation. This begins with the distinction between *hermeneutics* and the closely related word *exegesis*. While both words have to do with interpretation, they are not synonyms.

Defining Hermeneutics

Our word *hermeneutics* is from the Greek *hermeneia,* meaning interpretation or translation. Its root is the name of the god Hermes, who was the mythical divine messenger to humans.[1] The broadest and simplest definition of the English word *hermeneutics* is the theory and practice of interpreting "texts."[2] Notice that I said "texts" rather than "books." Books are just one kind of text. Those who work in the area of hermeneutics often include, as types of texts, culture, people's life stories, and the stories that are important to communities. The interpretation of books requires consideration of more than what is on the pages. Elements *outside* the book, but connected to it, must also be interpreted to discern its meaning. In terms of the Bible, we can say that to understand the Bible more fully, we must consider not only texts, but also contexts. The recognized biblical contexts are the historical, the theological, and the literary.

Hermeneutics involves all of these contexts. *The Oxford Dictionary of the Christian Church* provides a formal set of definitions of hermeneutics as used among theologians and Bible scholars. Hermeneutics is, "the wider study of how biblical faith may be conveyed in the language of fundamentally different civilizations."[3] Not only does this involve issues of translation, but it also requires considerations of culture, mores, social practices, and the like. If you have preached or taught a Church school Bible class, then you know how challenging the hermeneutic task can be. You know that there are many moments of interpretation that occur long before a sermon is preached or the lesson given. Hermeneutics is about interpreting the message of the Bible, or given texts within it, for today's listeners. It is about finding meaning in it for you and for me, and for the communities where we read, listen to, dialogue with, and live out our Christian discipleship.

In order for there to be sound hermeneutics in preaching and teaching, there must be competent *exegesis*.

Defining Exegesis

The word *exegesis* is from the Greek "to lead out" and refers to meaning. But, as you might expect, there is more to the idea and the practice than a simple basic definition indicates. Preaching and teaching are not only about the meaning of Bible texts for today; they are about what the texts meant in the times and places they were written. In order to apply the meaning of a biblical text to the present, the preacher must understand, as well as possible, what it may have meant in its original community or communities. According to the *Oxford Dictionary of the Christian Church*, "Whereas exegesis is usually the act of explaining a text . . . hermeneutics is the science or art by which exegetical procedures are devised."[4] Based on the first part of this definition, we may say that exegesis is the set of procedures an interpreter practices in order to determine a text's meaning. I believe Christian sermons ought to be grounded in sound exegesis of a biblical text.

Here is an example of exegesis compared with hermeneutics. When you are preparing to teach or preach, you may compare translations to see how various translators render a verse. Then you may consult commentaries to see what Bible scholars say about the differences among the translations, what may be known about the history of the development of the text and how that history may help you to understand its meaning for its original audience, insofar as that can be discerned. You may then consider the setting of the author and how the author's time and place in history may have contributed to the way she or he shaped the material.

For example, the Gospel of John begins with the phrase "In the beginning was the Word." The Greek word *logos*, which is translated "word" in this verse, was used by philosophers in ways that help us to understand something of what the author of that Gospel might have been trying to say and not to say to his readers about Jesus the Christ. This is exegesis, and it is upon such methods that conscientious preachers and teachers base their interpretations of the meaning of biblical texts and apply that meaning for today.

The rules for applying a biblical text's meanings for today are what guide hermeneutics. One such rule is not to let your own agenda determine how you apply the biblical text; another is never to violate the literary type or genre you are interpreting, and there are still others. If I were to apply a psalm of lament, where the psalmist is cursing his enemies, as justification for making war, I would be violating two firm hermeneutic principles, because I would be pressing the emotional self-expression of the psalmist into the service of my agenda.

But the second half of the definition of exegesis above suggests that there is more to hermeneutics than finding meaning responsibly for today's listeners: "hermeneutics is the science or art by which exegetical procedures are devised." This indicates that, while hermeneutics is based on sound exegesis, there is a sense in which sound exegesis is based on hermeneutics. In other words, as the study of the interpretation of texts, hermeneutics also is the theory about whether and how meaning is conveyed through texts and whose meaning it is that I articulate when I interpret the Bible. The problem is that when we ask what the original hearers thought or what the author or editors meant to say we are asking questions that cannot finally be answered with absolute confidence. It sometimes is easier to speak of what authors did not intend than it is to speak confidently about what they did intend.

This perennial problem notwithstanding, the following distinction generally holds true. If exegesis is about discerning a text's meaning in its own time and place, then hermeneutics is about drawing meaning from the text for today. A preacher's primary task when delivering a sermon is hermeneutic: to make sense of the biblical text in a way that will speak to the lives of those who will hear the sermon. Hermeneutics must be based on sound exegesis — sound methods of discerning the meanings of texts in contexts. However, there is a sense in which exegesis must be based on sound hermeneutics (a sound theory of meaning and its communication), hermeneutics, that is, as explained in the second part of our definition of exegesis. In other words, I must understand something of the dynamics of deriving meaning from language and texts if I am to practice well-informed exegesis.

Now let's see how some scholars exegete a passage that is crucial for answering the central question of this chapter: What did the earliest Christians believe about the inspiration of Bible? It may be that the most common and immediate answer given to this question is to quote 2 Timothy 3:16–17.

The Christian Testament on Inspiration

When you read 2 Timothy 3:16, "all Scripture is inspired by God," do you think of the entire Bible? Do you have a mental picture of God in relation to its authors and editors? Though these verses may seem clear and unambiguous at face value, they actually raise significant questions. First, what were the Scriptures to which the author, Paul, referred?[5] And second, what does Paul mean by "inspired by God?"

There is also a grammatical ambiguity that requires careful handling in the original Greek text. (This letter originally was written in the common Greek of the Greco-Roman world, which is called *koine*, pronounced coin-áy.) I will comment first on the grammatical ambiguity. This has a significant role in addressing our question, What were the Scriptures the author had in mind? The issue is whether verse 16 should be translated "all Scripture that is inspired is useful" or "all Scripture is inspired and useful."[6]

Here is an illustration of the difference. After I preach a sermon, a listener says, as she is leaving the church, "God really spoke to me through your sermon." I ask, "What in particular spoke to you?" She replies, "God spoke through all of it! I was mesmerized by your interpretation." I ask, "Does God speak to you through all of my sermons?" If the answer is yes (hallelujah!), then that person will have experienced the sermon like the second option for translating our text: "All Scripture is inspired."

A second person responds to my question this way: "God spoke through your jokes, but I did not hear God speaking in other parts of what you had to say." This corresponds to the first way of translating our ambiguous phrase: "All Scripture *that is* inspired is useful" (italics mine).

Bible scholar Paul Achtemeier offers helpful guidance on this. He concludes that, if the first translation holds true ("all Scripture that is inspired is useful"), then the author's intention clearly was not to focus on the inspiration of the Bible, but rather, on the "continuing utility of Scripture for religious purposes."[7] In other words, the emphasis is on the profitability of attending to its guidance and not on the fact of Scripture's inspiration. According to this translation, the subject would not be Scripture itself, but rather, "the nature of Scripture for the purpose of aiding the Christian life." Based on this passage alone, we cannot, therefore, extend the affirmation of Scripture's inspiration or usefulness to science or history, but rather, to what the text lists as the objects of Scripture's value. It is valuable for "such religious matters as teaching, reproof, correction, and training in righteousness."[8]

But which rendering of the verse is correct? Is either clearly to be preferred?

As you might expect, there are those who dissent vigorously from Achtemeier's conclusion. For scholar Gleason Archer, the subject of the verse is Scripture: "All Scripture is inspired." His view is that this verse clearly means that Scripture is entirely trustworthy and without error because all of it is fully inspired by God.[9]

A second challenge for interpreting 2 Timothy 3:16–17 is the word translated "inspiration," or "God-breathed." The Greek word is *theopneustos*. The roots of this word are *theos*, meaning "God," and *pneuma*, meaning "breath," "wind," or "spirit."[10] You can see from this combination of roots why the word can be translated "God-breathed." Though the word *theopneustos* occurs in the literature of the Greco-Roman world, this is its only appearance in the Christian Testament. Basing their interpretation on the use of this word both here and outside the Bible, it seems to the editors of the *Theological Dictionary of the New Testament* (a widely respected dictionary of New Testament Greek)[11] that the author of 2 Timothy uses the word to distinguish between the sacred writings of the Jewish and Christian people on the one hand, and the sacred writings of other people on the other hand. This differentiation is made based on the idea that it was the only true God who breathed life into the biblical texts that Paul had in mind.

However, there is disagreement among scholars about how this "in-breathing" was accomplished, especially with reference to the role and identity of the human writers. (We will take up this issue in the next chapter.)[12]

Other Passages

A second critical passage for our work in this chapter is 2 Peter 1:20–21. Verse 20 is the crux of the problem: "First of all you must understand this, that no prophecy of Scripture is a matter of one's own interpretation, because no prophecy ever came by human will, but men and women moved by the Holy Spirit spoke from God." The author[13] is addressing two interrelated issues.

Peter is saying that those who deny Christ's coming spin myths based on inauthentic sources; those who affirm Christ's coming base their beliefs on biblical prophecy. Peter teaches that biblical prophecy is superior to what he clearly regards as "cleverly devised myths" (2 Pet. 1:16). Peter urges his readers to believe those who base their views on authentic biblical prophecy rather than on questionable myths.

Peter's demonstration of the strength of biblical prophecy is based on his beliefs about both the inspiration of the Hebrew prophets, and the inspiration of the reader. Achtemeier says "The passage intends to have the reader take the prophecy of the Hebrew Scriptures seriously as coming not from the prophets themselves, but rather from the impulse of God's Spirit."[14] The importance of divine inspiration does not end with the speaking prophet, however. True interpretation is the result of God's inspiration. The reader must also be inspired for God's Word to accomplish God's purpose in giving it. A lack of faith in God's inspiration, then and now, will likely lead a reader to an erroneous interpretation.

Archer draws a conclusion from 2 Peter 1:20 different than Achtemeier. He refers to the prophets of the Hebrew Scriptures in general, saying they were "moved by the Holy Spirit and thus [each prophet] produced in his own human words exactly what God intended him to say."[15] Archer is emphatic: "the distinction between the doctrinal-theological

and the historical-scientific drawn by some modern writers on this subject is completely foreign to the attitude of the New Testament authors
toward the Old."[16] Why? If God said it, it must be true, whatever the
subject matter. Of course, this begs the question: Did God say everything
that is written in the Bible? And do we understand the many parts of the
Bible as they originally were meant? How may we account for differing
interpretations among faithful, prayerful people?

Still a third passage is John 10:35. The crucial language here is the
phrase, "the Scripture cannot be annulled." This gets at the crucial question of Jesus' own attitude toward Scripture. In the passage where this
verse is contained, Jesus is challenged by his opponents. He had been
performing works of power; his opponents do not deny it. What they
challenge is Jesus' calling himself the Son of God. They accuse him of
blasphemy because to make such a claim is to claim to be divine, and
there is only one true God. Jesus' response is strategic. He refers to
Psalm 82:6 where the writer of that psalm refers to the children of Israel
as "gods." If the children of Israel are gods, then why are his opponents
challenging him? His opponents have no argument — Jesus is saying
nothing they have not heard, as educated Jews — and they have seen
his works of power. Why cannot he who is greater than the ancient
children of Israel designate himself in this way? Since to say otherwise
is to violate their own view of the Scriptures and to deny their own
approach to interpreting it, Jesus has put his opponents in checkmate.
In effect, Jesus used their methods against them. If they say he is wrong,
they call their own approach to Scripture false; if they do not persist in
challenging Jesus' claim to be God's Son, then he has won the argument.
Since what we have here is a strategy on Jesus' part that was employed
for a very specific circumstance, then, according to Achtemeier, we cannot use it to claim that Jesus necessarily is advocating his opponents'
understanding of, or way of interpreting, the Scriptures.[17]

Achtemeier summarizes his findings as follows. The authors of the
Christian Testament believed God was the source of the Hebrew Scriptures. The Scriptures, therefore, are to be taken seriously; but references
to and treatment of the Hebrew Scriptures by the authors of the Christian Testament are not "about verbal inerrancy, or errorlessness in

matters of secular interest."[18] The value and authority of the Hebrew Scriptures is the same as that of the Christian Testament. The chief value of the Bible is derived from the witness of its authors to the acts of God. According to Achtemeier, Jesus treats the Hebrew Scriptures with a sort of "sovereign disregard."[19] He says this is evident in that Jesus had a high view of the law but a loose way of interpreting it.

Again, Archer takes a different view. Of John 10:35 Archer writes, "He [Jesus] clearly presupposed that whatever the Old Testament taught was true because it was the infallible word of God."[20] Of 2 Peter 1:20, 21, Archer writes, "As they wrote down God's revelation, the Old Testament authors were supernaturally borne along (like sailing vessels impelled by the wind, *pheromenoi*) to record God's truth, which is not to be perverted by one's own personal interpretation or preference."[21] Archer's conclusion: "Both Christ and the apostles affirm, then, that what the Bible says, God says. . . . We can reject or evade its teaching only at the peril of our souls."[22] The kind of inerrancy the Bible claims, says Archer, extends to all matters, including historical and scientific.

The difference between Archer and Achtemeier is classic. It has much to do with the difference between deductive (beginning with a theory or belief) and inductive (beginning with the data) approaches to the Bible. Archer's method is deductive and anachronistic; Achtemeier applies a more inductive strategy. In the next chapter, I will consider further this difference and its implications, in light of the incarnational analogy for divine inspiration.

Back Now to Our Questions

What are the Scriptures to which Paul refers? The Scriptures with which Paul and Timothy would have been familiar, with just a few exceptions, were the collection of writings we call the Hebrew Scriptures, not the Christian Testament. It had not yet been collected.

Our second question was, What does it mean to say the Bible is inspired? Our answer is that it has a unique relationship to God as shepherd of the process of its development. God stirred those who wrote and edited what we have in the Bible, which is a view closer to Achtemeier's than Archer's.

But this begs further clarification. Did God overwhelm the humanity of the authors and editors of the Scriptures when God inspired them? Or did God work through their humanity in a way that accomplished the desired results — that expressed God's intentions? Still further, if the writers' humanity was intact, could the Bible be without any error at all? We turn to the next chapter with these questions in mind.

Summary

In this chapter we have defined *hermeneutics* and *exegesis*. Hermeneutics is the theory of interpretation behind specific methods of interpreting texts. As such, it involves how we relate meanings from one person, time and place to another. Exegesis is the method or step-by-step process by which we arrive at "original" meanings, insofar as they may be discerned.

We looked at what may be learned about the inspiration of the Bible from several passages in the Christian Testament. Our conclusion was that the key biblical proof-texts for the Bible's own inspiration are not so clearcut as some want them to be. To say that the Bible "claims" to be inspired by God as we now have it would be to commit the error of reading into texts what we want to hear from them. On the other hand, these verses clearly associate the Hebrew Scriptures with God's own work, and, I believe, it is significant that the Christian churches eventually called their own authoritative writings Scripture as well.

Questions for Discussion

◆ What is the relationship between hermeneutics and exegesis?

◆ What exegetical methods do you employ when you study the Bible?

◆ Do your exegetical methods correlate with, or reflect, your beliefs about the Bible?

◆ Describe your understanding or interpretation of the statement: God inspired the entire Bible.

◆ Do you believe the Bible attests explicitly to its own divine inspiration? Why? Or why not?

Notes

1. "Hermeneut," *Shorter Oxford English Dictionary on Historic Principles* (Oxford: Clarendon Press, 1933), 894.

2. Kevin Vanhoozer defines "text" as "a communicative act of a communicative agent fixed in writing." This definition reflects his work with speech-act theory; *Is There a Meaning in This Text? The Bible, the Reader, and the Morality of Literary Knowledge* (Grand Rapids: Zondervan, 1998), 225.

3. *Oxford Dictionary of the Christian Church*, rev. 2nd ed., ed. F. L. Cross and E. A. Livingstone (Oxford: Oxford University Press, 1958, 1983), 641.

4. Ibid.; from the Greek *exageomai*, "I narrate, explain." Exegesis has to do with drawing the meaning out of a text (ibid., 490).

5. Many scholars have concluded that a group of the apostle Paul's followers continued to write in his name even after his death. Not all scholars agree that the Pastoral Epistles were written by someone other than the apostle Paul. John A. T. Robinson discusses these issues in *Re-dating the New Testament* (Philadelphia: Westminster Press, 1976). I do not ascribe to his theory that pivots on the fall of Jerusalem, but his discussions are informative.

6. Paul Achtemeier discusses this question in *The Inspiration of Scripture: Biblical Perspectives on Current Issues*, ed. Howard Clark Kee (Philadelphia: Westminster Press, 1980), 106–7.

7. Ibid., 107.

8. Ibid.

9. Gleason L. Archer, "The Witness of the Bible to Its Own Inerrancy," in *The Foundation of Biblical Authority*, ed. James Montgomery Boice (Grand Rapids: Zondervan, 1978), 85–99.

10. UBS Greek New Testament, dictionary, 145.

11. "theopneustos" in Geoffrey Bromley, trans. and ed., *Theological Dictionary of the New Testament*, vol. 4, German ed. Gerhard Friedrich (Grand Rapids: Eerdmans, 1968), 453–55.

12. B. B. Warfield, *The Inspiration and Authority of the Bible* (Philadelphia: Presbyterian and Reformed Publishing Co., 1948), 245–96, made much of the idea that this word must be interpreted as if the God breathes out from or through the Scriptures and into us.

13. Some do not believe Peter the Apostle wrote this letter. Refer to my earlier n. 5 on the authorship of 2 Timothy for a parallel explanation.

14. Achtemeier, *The Inspiration of Scripture*, 110.

15. Archer, "The Witness of the Bible to Its Own Inerrancy," 90.
16. Ibid., 91.
17. Achtemeier, *The Inspiration of Scripture,* 111.
18. Ibid., 112.
19. Ibid., 113.
20. Archer, "The Witness of the Bible to Its Own Inerrancy," 94.
21. Ibid., 95.
22. Ibid.

Chapter Six

Stirred How?

THE PULSATING HEART of the Christian faith is the belief that Jesus Christ was and is the personal revelation of God. He was and is the revealer of God and of God's will for our lives as individuals and as communities of Christian people. As I write this, every way I think of to describe Jesus Christ seems an understatement. God as ultimate reality — that is, Reality as such — is a theme in the writings of C. S. Lewis. It is that Reality that has visited us in Christ Jesus.[1] Since Christians believe God has come in person, we are not, finally, people of a book. There no longer need be any doubt about God's will toward us because God's Word is action in Jesus of Nazareth, and God the Holy Spirit abides with us.[2]

And yet we must admit that we know of Jesus Christ principally through a book. There is much that we would not know about Jesus if there were no Bible. Among the Hebrew Scriptures we have pointers to Christ's identity that helped the early Church to verify and to comprehend what it means to call Jesus Messiah and Lord. In the Christian Testament we have the tradition-affirmed apostolic witnesses to Jesus the Messiah.

The affirmation of faith that the Bible is unique because God the Holy Spirit inspired its formation leads to yet another question: How did God inspire the writers and editors of the Bible? Did God dictate to those who wrote and guide the choices of those who edited the stories and documents that are in the Bible? Or did God respect the identity and humanity of those the Spirit moved to bear witness to God?

There is a spectrum of possible answers to these questions.

Four Views of Biblical Inspiration

The diagram on the following page — which elaborates on a model used by Joseph Manley Hopkins, my Old Testament professor at Westminster College, New Wilmington, Pennsylvania, more than thirty years ago — will help explain the main points of view on the spectrum of options.

Arrow number 1 represents the belief that the Bible is inspired in the way that, let's say, Shakespeare was inspired. I call this the "general inspiration" of Scripture. According to this view the Bible is fully a human work; God did not inspire it in any direct sense. The biblical writers wrote when "the muse" (Greek deities of artistic inspiration), rather than the Holy Spirit, "was upon them."

In this view, the Bible should be approached like any other book that has had culture-shaping influence. After all, The Bible has numerous characteristics in common with other books or ancient texts. It contains inconsistencies and apparent contradictions, and there are variants among the manuscripts. Readers who take this view of inspiration are likely to employ an inductive, to be distinguished from a deductive, method of assessing the evidence from the Bible about the Bible.

For example, a reader discovers that there are differences among the Gospels. The wording and the ordering of the stories they have in common are sometimes inconsistent. The Gospel of John, for instance, places the cleansing of the temple on the day of Christ's triumphant entry into Jerusalem at the beginning of Christ's ministry. The other Gospels place it much later. In acknowledging this, the reader's understanding of biblical inspiration begins to change. It is becoming more inductive; that is, he or she begins to look at what is in the text and then draws conclusions about the Bible based on what is there. A deductive approach makes assumptions first and then approaches the text in light of them. A deductive approach might reason that, since the Bible is accurate in every detail, the contradictions are in the way a reader interprets them. Readers might then put a great deal of effort into resolving "apparent contradictions."

Many differences of detail such as these appear in the Bible. These, along with other textual problems, are cited as justifications for the

The Inspiration and Authority of Scripture

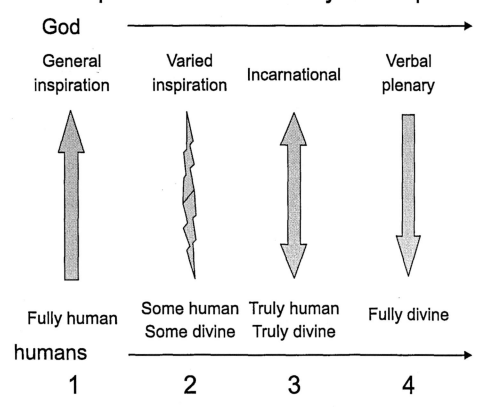

general inspiration point of view about the very human nature of the Bible. Humans, however, are not capable of a purely inductive or a purely deductive approach to learning. Those who begin "from below" also bring assumptions to the process of interpretation, and an approach that leans toward the inductive does not necessarily render one's view of the Bible "low."[3]

According to "varied inspiration," number 2 on our diagram, some passages are included in the Bible by God's will. Others are not. Inspiration is like an uneven landscape. Even where the inspired parts of Scripture are concerned, some passages are inspired differently than others, and for different purposes. This is reflected in the liturgical invitation to "listen for," instead of "listen to" the Word of God.

The distinction between aspects that are and are not inspired by God can sometimes be arbitrary from the varied inspiration perspective. That is not to say that readers who take this view are not thoughtful and discerning. Discussing this issue, one of my students, for example, pointed out that "certain parts of the Bible are more or less related to Christ and, hence [more or less immediately instructive], for Christians."[4] In my opinion, the entire Bible is intended by God for our instruction, but inspiration correlates with genre and discernible intention, and to determine this sometimes requires vigorous wrestling with the texts in their contexts.

Arrow number 4 points downward. The belief that God guided every word of the writers of Scripture is frequently referred to as "verbal plenarism." You know the word *verbal*: It comes from the Latin *verbum*, meaning "word." The root of the word *plenary* is the Latin *plene*, which means full. In this view, God not only inspired the writers, but God fully inspired them. In the strictest verbal plenary view, every word is God's Word, and every jot, tittle, and dash in Scripture is meant by God to be there.

The perspective of verbal plenary inspiration is justified by the belief that the Bible attests to its own inspiration. It is in this sense self-authenticating. The key texts that testify to this conclusion, among others, are the ones we considered in the previous chapter: 2 Timothy 3:16, 2 Peter 1:20–21, and John 10:35. In the latter verse, the way Jesus treated the Hebrew Scriptures is the focal point. In this approach the Bible is interpreted deductively, which is to say the interpreter adheres to a theology of the Bible into which the facts must be fit. Gleason Archer, quoted earlier, approached the Bible from this kind of perspective. Paul Achtemeier did not.

When they encounter problems with the text, interpreters from the verbal plenary perspective are forced to try to reconcile differences. In the end they are forced to acknowledge that their belief in the verbal and historical inerrancy of Scripture is based on assumptions about the so-called "autographs" — the original biblical texts. None of these are extant, so there is great effort to reconstruct them. This process raises yet other questions. Multiple authors and editors created some books of the Bible. At which point in that long process did the text become inerrant? We are left with the texts we have in hand; it is *their* status that is most relevant to us here and now.

As I have said since early on in this book, I prefer the "incarnational" view of biblical inspiration (number 3 on the diagram). According to this view, the Bible is to be understood as incarnational in a way that is analogous to the Incarnation of the Word in Jesus the Christ.[5] There is a connection between Christ the Word and the Scriptures: Christ is the Word to which the Scriptures as a whole bear witness (though not in every detail), and through the Holy Spirit Christ the Word uses the Scriptures to bear witness to God.

The incarnational view of the Bible affirms that the manner in which the scriptural message has been preserved is in itself intended by God to teach us something. That something is that God does not violate our humanity — by, for example, treating us as if we are hand-puppets, with no personal history, contexts, or points of view of our own — in order to communicate with us, just as, in orthodox Christian thought, the Incarnation did not violate the human whom God the Eternally Begotten became.[6]

On the other hand, those through whom God spoke did not impede the divine purposes for their inspiration, just as the humanity of Jesus did not pollute the Word made flesh. We can observe, then, that incarnationalists are plenarists, of a sort. They are not, however, verbal plenarists. They do not believe God guided the word choices of the writers and editors of the Holy Scripture. They also share traits with varied inspirationists, believing that the inspiration of the Bible is like an uneven landscape, with depth, texture and a plethora of diversity.[7] That diversity must be considered fully when listening for God. Still, in its diversity, the Bible is one, unified, through God's inspiration of it. The whole Bible is inspired and used by God to shape us into the people God intends us to be.

The incarnationalist understands inspiration to be "from above" — from the transcendent God — but it involves the full participation of immanent sources, which God the Spirit uses "from below." The texts express the humanity of their authors, including personal experience, idiosyncrasies, and contexts.

Rightly considered, contexts serve rather than inhibit the communication of meaning. While contexts do not fully determine meaning, they are vital aspects of meaning. Form cannot be separated from content any more than content can be divorced from form. As I said, humanness was not overwhelmed in this expression (or incarnation) of God's Word.

Notice that I said "God's Word" rather than "God's words." We must keep clearly in mind that the Bible is only the penultimate expression of God's speech, and that only Christ is ultimate. Only Christ was God.

We must beware of reversing the incarnational analogy. Christ is not like the Bible. While the Bible was inspired like the Word was incarnate in Christ, Christ is not like the Bible. (Reversing the analogy presses it too far.)

Where and in Whom Inspiration Occurs

Readers who hold an incarnational view of the Bible struggle with questions of language and meaning. Was it the writers and editors, or is it the writings themselves, that are inspired? Is the inspiration of the text meaningful if the reader is not also inspired by the Holy Spirit to interpret it?

There has been much discussion about the relationships among language, texts, authors, and readers. Of course, it is beyond the scope of this book to engage thoroughly the issues at stake, even if philosophical hermeneutics were my specialty. Without pretending to be thorough about it, I may, nevertheless, present the basic issues in an introductory way by starting with these questions: Whose meaning do I conceptualize when I read a book? The author's? The text's? My own or my community's? Or is meaning more complex than an either/or answer can account for?

The philosophers and theologians who have wrestled with these questions include the "postmodern" philosopher-linguists Jacques Derrida and Roland Barthes. Postmodern theologians who engage this subject include Mark C. Taylor, James McClendon, and David Tracy.[8] Though there are variations on their themes, the gist of their work as it relates to biblical inspiration is that we never can get at the meaning an author intended to inscribe when writing. So the inspiration of the author is, finally, irrelevant.

They note that authors do not necessarily write what they intend to say — what they really mean. You probably have had the experience of proofreading something you have written, only to find that you did not write quite what you "meant to say," or as clearly as you thought you had written it.

Furthermore, neither authors' intentions, nor the form and content of their work, determine readers' interpretations. Note how often readers derive meaning from a book that the author says she or he did not intend. In fact, postmodern thinkers assert that readers really determine the meanings of texts.

Here is an illustration of what they say. We all bring our life experiences to the act of interpretation. I say to a group, "God is love," and we discuss what that means. I discover that there are many ways to understand how God is love. We each understand it according to our experience with the giving and receiving of love in our families and communities. That is the context of our interpretation of the verse. But since our experiences cannot be identical with our neighbor's — even siblings have different experiences with a parent's love — there really is not a discernible single, constant meaning in the text "God is love."

What, then, is to keep us from saying just any conceivable interpretation is possible?

For the postmodern, the reader's community is a hedge against entirely freewheeling interpretation. Since we live in particular communities, each with its own culture, our interpretations bear our culture's stamp. The interpretation of a text is always what we believe the words mean, but that conclusion is shaped by our experience in our communities, comprehended through language as used in our community.

The incarnational analogy enables us to appreciate and critique postmodern thinking as it relates to our faith, both in God's inspiration of the Scriptures and the Holy Spirit's inspiration of us as we interpret it. We will discuss this in part 3. Suffice it to say, for now, that words and texts have meaning that transcends specific times and places. After all, when I say with the author of 1 John that God is love (4:8), people in all times and places have understood at least the core, perhaps the heart, of what that means.[9] Communication happens! And it happens across times and between and among cultures.

Back to the Question

Recall now our earlier question: How did God inspire the writers and editors of the Bible, and those who interpret it? Our answer is that God moved them in a way that respected them fully as human beings and utilized their humanity and contexts in the service of God's Word. They are not errorless, but their errors are innocuous with respect to the truth God intends to teach us through the Bible. In the same way, if Jesus made human errors — bending nails or measuring wrong as a carpenter — that would not have diluted the truth of his life, teaching, and saving work. Christ thirsted, and Christ walked on water. In both, he was "very human and very God."

Our next questions are, What did this process look like? How did the Bible come to be as we have it? And what was God's role in that formative process?

Summary

We noted again that the Bible is Christianity's primary source for faith in Jesus Christ, who was and is God's self-revelation to our world.

We described the range of views among Christians about God's involvement in the writing and shaping of the Bible. "General inspiration" is the view that the Bible is inspired like any other book and should be interpreted like any other. "Varied inspiration" takes the view that the Bible contains inspiration, but inspiration occurs in varying ways and for varying purposes. The "verbal plenary" view holds that the entire Bible is fully and thoroughly inspired, so that it contains the words God wanted to be there. Finally, there is the incarnational view. Incarnationalists are plenarists of a sort, but they are quite clear that the humanity of the writers of the Bible, influenced as they were by their histories and contexts, was in no way compromised by God's use of them, nor was God's purpose in using them compromised by their humanity.

Questions for Discussion

◆ Which of the four ways of thinking about biblical inspiration described in this chapter best expresses your own beliefs about the Bible?

◆ When you think about the authors and editors of the Bible in the act of writing, how do you picture God in relation to them? How does God influence them?

◆ When you think about the authors of the Bible, do you think about them as holier than others? Or were they just ordinary folks whom God decided to use?

◆ When you introduce a quote from the Bible do you say, "St. Paul [or, whoever] said"? Or do you introduce a quote from the Bible with the words "God says"?

Further Reading

Brauch, Manfred T. *Abusing Scripture: The Consequences of Misreading the Bible.* Downers Grove, Ill.: InterVarsity Press Academic, 2009.

Green, Joel. *Seized by Truth: Reading the Bible as Scripture.* Nashville: Abingdon, 2007.

Gorman, Michael, ed. *Scripture: An Ecumenical Introduction to the Bible and Its Interpretation.* Peabody, Mass.: Hendrickson Publishers, 2005.

Peterson, Eugene H. *Eat This Book.* Grand Rapids: Eerdmans, 2006.

Segovia, Fernando F., and Mary Tolbert, eds. *Reading from This Place.* Vol. 1. Minneapolis: Fortress Press, 1995.

———. *Reading from this Place.* Vol. 2. Minneapolis: Fortress Press, 1995.

Vanhoozer, Keven. *Is There a Meaning in This Text? The Bible, the Reader, and the Morality of Literary Knowledge.* Grand Rapids: Zondervan, 1998.

Vanhoozer, Keven, James K. A. Smith, and Bruce Ellis Benson, eds. *Hermeneutics at the Crossroads.* Bloomington: Indiana University Press, 2006.

Notes

1. For example, C. S. Lewis, *The Problem of Pain* (New York: Collier Macmillan, 1962), 24–25.

2. Karl Barth, *God in Action,* trans. Elmer G. Homrighausen and Karl J. Ernst (Manhasset, N.Y.: Round Table Press, 1963).

3. D. M. Beegle, *The Inspiration of Scripture* (Philadelphia: Westminster Press, 1963), 11–16. This work was expanded considerably in Beegle's, *Scripture, Tradition and Infallibility* (Grand Rapids: Eerdmans, 1973).

4. A very excellent former student of mine, Christopher Klopp, offered this thought during a feedback session on a very early draft of this paragraph.

5. According to Alister McGrath, this paradigm had broad implications for John Calvin; see *A Life of John Calvin: A Study in the Shaping of Western Culture* (Grand Rapids: Baker [Blackwell], 1990, 1995), 149. Several recent studies have worked this out in connection with hermeneutics. They are listed among recommended reading for part 2. I am especially impressed with the work of Jeannine K. Brown, *Scripture as Communication: Introducing Biblical Hermeneutics* (Grand Rapids: Baker Academic, 2007). Reading her book should be the very next step students of this subject take in their study of biblical hermeneutics.

6. Manfred T. Brauch has recently unpacked this analogy in *Abusing Scripture: The Consequences of Misreading the Bible* (Downers Grove, Ill.: InterVarsity Press Academic, 2009), 25–32.

7. Dr. William Jacobsen was the first I heard use this language. It was during a conversation in the Koinonia Café at Palmer Theological Seminary in Wynnewood, Pennsylvania. I do not remember exactly when.

8. Kevin Vanhoozer, "Theology and the Condition of Postmodernity: A Report of Knowledge (of God)," *The Cambridge Companion to Postmodern Theology*, ed. K. J. Vanhoozer (Cambridge: Cambridge University Press, 2003), 19–20.

9. Vanhoozer's work in general is in critical and respectful dialogue with postmodern hermeneutics, e.g., *Is There a Meaning in This Text? The Bible, the Reader, and the Morality of Literary Knowledge* (Grand Rapids: Zondervan, 1998); and Kevin Vanhoozer, James K. A. Smith, and Bruce Ellis Benson, eds., *Hermeneutics at the Crossroads* (Bloomington: Indiana University Press, 2006).

Part III

Canon

Case Study: The Teenager's Doubts

A sixteen-year-old recently committed his life to Christ. He loves reading the Bible, but finds many passages difficult to understand. With the enthusiasm of a new convert, he perseveres, and of course has many questions. You, his Church school teacher, are one of the people he relies on for help with the questions the Bible provokes. One day he seems very unsettled. You ask what is troubling him. He says he has found an error in the Bible. He discovered that Mark's Gospel has an alternate ending, and the famous story of the woman caught in adultery is not in the earliest manuscripts of John's Gospel. The young man's inquisitive mind cascades with questions, which he shares with you: "How did the Bible come to be? Were the books of the Bible pieced together, or were they written all at once? Who decided it should be the authority for our faith and life?" The young man is beginning to wonder if we really can trust it. "If we can't trust the Bible, then how can we know anything about God and God's will for us?"

Chapter Seven

Telling and Writing

THE YOUNG PERSON in our case likely would not have faced a crisis of faith if he had known more about how the books of the Bible came to be as they are. An incarnational view of the Bible's formation opens up possibilities for a more balanced way of understanding God's relationship to the Bible. An incarnational viewpoint acknowledges God's Word at work in the speaking, hearing, writing, and collecting of the books in the Bible. It demonstrates God's profound respect for, and intention to use, the humanity of those whom God inspired to write. It sees revelation by way of both inductive and deductive methods. It places the transcendent with the immanent: revelation comes from above through the full participation of what is below. An incarnational understanding helps us to interpret theologically the development of Scripture as God's shepherding of the very human process of canonization. Shepherds guide and nurture sheep. They do not control their every move. They direct their paths, not their every step. This way of understanding the development of the canon of Christian Scriptures is the subject of this third part of our study.

The question that will govern this chapter will address the root of the dilemma of the young person in our case: How did the individual documents or books of the Bible come to be as they are? In order to answer this, we must first make a distinction between direct and indirect authorship.

Authorship

If God guided the writers of the Bible to the degree that the authors wrote exactly what God wanted them to write, then the human writers were merely scribes and God was the Bible's author. Conversely, if the writers, editors, and collectors of the documents of the Bible contributed substantively not only to the form but also to the contents of the Bible, then they were the direct or immediate authors of the Bible, and God's Word is related to the Bible indirectly.

It seems clear to me that the Bible contains many kinds of books that are the work of many authors and have multiple perspectives. As we shall see, some of them do not accommodate the idea of a single author, even when a single individual is named as the author.

Many Kinds of "Books"

Bookstores and libraries offer books on an wide range of subjects: history, philosophy, sociology, literature, and so forth. Of course, you will find the Bible in the religion section. There are characteristic themes and ways of writing associated with every subject, and within each subject there are subtopics and themes. The history section includes books on American, French, and German history, to name just three examples. Every subject has such subtopics.

Literature books are divided into genres. Webster's first definition of genre is, "a category of artistic, musical, or literary composition characterized by a particular style, form, or content."[1] Poetry is one genre, historical novel is another, romance novel is another, and so on. Each of these is a way of writing literature. There are many literary genres in the Bible.

You will recognize varieties of subjects, themes, and genres in the following list of biblical books. Among them are history-like books:[2] Genesis, Exodus, Joshua, 1 and 2 Samuel, 1 and 2 Kings, 1 and 2 Chronicles, Ezra, Nehemiah, the Acts of the Apostles, and the Gospels. There are books of social organization and law: Numbers, Deuteronomy, and Leviticus. Among the books where wisdom is the theme are Proverbs, Ecclesiastes, and Job. The great poetic book of the Bible is, of course, the Book of Psalms; Song of Songs is yet another. There are epistles (letters) by Peter, Jude, James, Paul, John, or their followers. The great

apocalypse is the Book of the Revelation of Jesus Christ to John (apocalyptic literature disguises what it reveals in highly symbolic imagery),
but Daniel, Ezekiel, and Matthew contain apocalyptic passages too.
The books of the prophets are well known: Isaiah, Jeremiah, Lamen-
tations, Ezekiel, Daniel, Hosea, Zephaniah, Habakkuk, Amos, Obadiah,
Nahum, Zachariah, and Malachi. The Gospels are Matthew, Mark, Luke,
and John.

Inspiration comes to each genre in its own way. If you ever have
written poetry and prose, you know a different stirring leads to each. If
you have had writer's block, you know that to continue writing biogra-
phy requires different inspiration than that required to continue writing
science or history. The genre shapes the process of writing and what is
written. Each subject is engaged in its own way.

I said above that the books of the Bible that tell us what happened
are history-like. When we twenty-first-century Christians refer to books
of history, we refer to books that aim to present as objective an account
and interpretation of events as possible. This was not the case with the
writing of ancient history. The writers and compilers of 1 and 2 Kings,
for example, seem to have been as interested in meaning as in facts.
Though they were not unconcerned about events as such (they were
not writing fiction), they wrote with an eye toward conveying meaning
through the way they told the story. Baillie remarks that "revelation is
always given us through events; yet not all events, but only through such
as appear to us as God's mighty works; and through no event in its bare
character as occurrence, but only as men [and women] are enabled by
the Spirit of God to apprehend and receive its revelatory power."[3]

One difference between ancient and modern history telling is the
idea of a single author. Modern histories are by and large written by
individual authors or identifiable groups of persons. The writers gather
evidence and treat their sources as objectively as possible. Sources must
be properly credited and plagiarism avoided. The work of a historian is
considered to be more convincing insofar as it seems to be unbiased.

Not so in the ancient world. The ancients were more tolerant of
the subjective dimension of history telling. The details provided by the
teller helped convey the meaning of the story. They did not observe the

distinction between fact and purpose, or meaning, that is so integral to modern methods.[4] This is not to say that there is no history behind the biblical stories, nor that the early keepers of the community memory did not tell about events as they saw them, but their stories are history-like, rather than historical in the modern sense of the word.

Remembering these two facts — that the biblical authors were not expected to be objective in the sense that modern historians are, and that there are multiple points of view even when trying to preserve the memory of events — will help us understand the history-like books of the Bible.

Many people, for example, assert that Moses is the single author of the first five books of the Bible (also called the Pentateuch or Torah). Many biblical scholars think it is more likely that these early historical books of the Bible developed first by the telling and retelling of the stories that the people of Israel found most meaningful — their culture-shaping stories. These stories were eventually written down, edited, and reedited in light of the most current circumstances the people were facing. In other words, the so-called "historical books" of the Bible came to their present shape by way of a very long and human process.

For example, some of the stories in Genesis have parallels elsewhere in the Fertile Crescent (modern Iraq through Palestine and Egypt) that originated before and during the time of early biblical formation.[5] Even those who believe Moses wrote the Pentateuch must allow that he included material inherited from other tribes and cultures.

One of these stories is about a great flood. It is found among many different groups of people around the world. Though details differ, these narratives are based on a common, ancient one that is older than the biblical text and more ancient than writing itself. The inclusion of the story of the great flood in Genesis demonstrates how traditional material transmitted by word of mouth was later used by the author and editors of Genesis for their purposes.

Bible scholars identify many layers of material in the first five books of the Bible and propose theories about the long-term editing of the Hebrew Scriptures. One theory, for example, is the famous (in some circles infamous) Documentary Hypothesis.

According to this theory, a series of so-called "redactors of the original material" shaped the texts. (A redactor is a kind of editor with a theological purpose. I will discuss this further in chapter 11.) These redactors represent different times, places, life-settings, and points of view. According to the hypothesis, perhaps as many as four traditions of redaction are detectable in the Pentateuch, each with its own emphasis and concerns: the Yahwist, Elohist, Deuteronomic, and the Priestly traditions.[6]

An example from family life will illustrate how community storytellers may have preserved and developed the earliest parts of Genesis, Exodus, and other narrative sections of the Bible.

Most families have stories that are told from generation to generation. Parents and grandparents often enjoy telling their grandchildren the stories that their parents and grandparents told them.

Suppose that your grandmother and her sister are the family storytellers — the "lore-keepers." They like to tell an entertaining story about the time their grandmother did something that made a huge difference in her neighbor's life. They agree about some of the details, but disagree about others. They do agree about the story's value and why it should be told. It demonstrates that their grandmother was a person to be admired for her generosity. That event shaped their imaginations and, in turn, the way they lived their lives. By telling you that story, they hope to preserve the testimony to their grandmother's character and to inspire you to be a generous person.

Years later, you tell the same story to your grandchildren. They ask about the details. You have done your best to remember the story accurately, but there were, after all, differences between the versions told by the two women. Furthermore, your grandchildren's questions reflect interest in aspects of the story that did not interest you and your generation. So you must interpret the details in order to address their questions. Furthermore, you believe your grandchildren need to learn a lesson of faithfulness from your great-grandmother's example. You want the narrative of her life to shape their imaginations, so you tell the story in a way that draws out the point quite clearly.

Suppose you write these stories down, and generations from now someone finds them in an old desk drawer. Your great, great grandson reads it, treats it with reverence, thinks about the way the family is at the time, the values they hold dear, and gives thanks for your great-grandmother's example. He shares it with other family members, who compare it with versions they have heard. Call one source "J" for Aunt Jenny, and another "B" for Aunt Bessie. Together they contribute to a greater whole, and the process goes on and on.

A very similar kind of development can be seen in the books that were intended to preserve the history of Israel. Looking at those books and the Gospels in particular, we see that there is more than one perspective on many of the events and subjects encountered in the Bible.

Many Points of View

The stories of the lives and times of Israel and Judah during the reigns of their kings beyond Saul, David, and Solomon are narrated in two sets of books: 1 and 2 Kings and 1 and 2 Chronicles. Their points of view are not the same. Likewise, each Gospel has its own point of view on the life and teaching of Jesus of Nazareth. Matthew, Mark, and Luke collected, arranged, and commented on the material in the Gospels that bear their names. They used a range of sources. The Gospels of Matthew and Luke seem to be based principally on three sources. One is the Gospel of Mark; another is a source Luke and Matthew have in common that Mark did not use (and probably did not know), which consists primarily of sayings of Jesus. Many scholars of the Christian Testament call this source "Q" from the German word *Quelle*, meaning "source." Third, Matthew and Luke have material that is unique to them. All three wrote from different perspectives, for different audiences. Their concerns influenced their choices of sources and their selection of details.

In the case of the Gospels, I believe no one writer's point of view could have been sufficient to bear the weight of what was being revealed: "the glory as of a father's only son" (John 1:14). Their interpretation and history writing could not bear the weight of the meaning of the moment; only telling the story would do. Nevertheless, the Gospel writers also wanted to tell what happened. They did that from their unique points of view.

Please note that I am not saying there is no history behind the stories told in Scripture. Its authors, writers, and editors certainly intended to tell what happened. The telling was, as it always is, from the perspective of the teller. Historians tell us cultures dependent on oral tradition were remarkably able to transmit accurately the teachings and metaphors they valued. The quality of their faithfulness in passing on the history of their people should not be underestimated.[7]

Back to Our Questions

How did the books of the Bible come to be as they are today? Some were written substantially, though not exactly, as we have them (e.g., many of the letters of Paul, and the history-like book of Acts.)[8] Others developed by a longer, dialogical process among witnesses, responders to witnesses, and editors.

What I am saying is that God shepherded the composition of the books of the Bible by a very organic process that respected people in their times and places, through numerous genres and generations. The crucial matter is our belief that God shepherded the process. I believe God continues to shepherd interpretations of Scripture, weaving a dynamic and lively tapestry of faithfulness among the communities that interpret it. While we cannot point to a time when the Spirit was not at work, there was a pivotal period of authoritative preservation of the apostolic witness through Scripture. And this brings us back to tradition and the relationship between the Bible and tradition, which is at the heart of any consideration of the canon of Scripture and its formation. It is to the collecting of the canon that we will turn in the next chapter.

Summary

There are many kinds of writing and literary genres in the Bible. There is poetry and law, prophecy, history, wisdom, and so on.

Some books of the Bible originated as written documents, e.g. the Pauline Epistles.

The idea of proprietary individual authorship as we know it does not apply to the Scriptures. The authorial names attached to various texts (Matthew, Paul, and others) do not necessarily signify that a single author is responsible for everything in the text.

Parts of both the Hebrew and the Christian Scriptures did not originate as written texts. They began as oral tradition, eventually put to writing and edited over time.

There is a sense in which the historical books in the Bible had many authors and editors, including editors who made substantive adjustments and additions to what they had received.

Our efforts to write objective history would be foreign to the ways biblical authors narrated events. It is not that they were unconcerned with telling what happened, but they told history as story with conscious interest in passing on meaning.

In many cases the Bible includes more than one point of view on the same events and their meanings. This can be said of other content as well. For example: Proverbs and Ecclesiastes are both about wisdom, but they do not share the same point of view in every case.

Questions for Discussion

♦ Do you believe Moses wrote the first five books of the Bible? Why or why not?

♦ Would the Bible still be the final, not the sole, authority and guide of your faith and behavior if it is true that the documents in it were edited over a long period of time?

♦ What are the implications of the fact that there is more than one point of view on the same events in the Bible? Does this undermine or strengthen your belief in the Bible's authenticity?

♦ Why do different literary genres require different ways of inspiration?

♦ Imagine the work of a shepherd. How do you see God's guiding of the formation of Scripture to be similar to that? Different?

Notes

1. *Merriam-Webster's Collegiate Dictionary*, 2007, s.v. "genre."

2. I associate this language with narrative theology. See Hans Frei, *The Eclipse of Biblical Narrative: A Study in Eighteenth- and Nineteenth- Century Hermeneutics* (New Haven, Conn.: Yale University Press, 1974); George Lindbeck, *The Nature of Doctrine: Religion and Theology in a Postliberal Age* (Philadelphia: Westminster Press, 1984).

3. John Baillie, *The Idea of Revelation in Recent Thought* (New York: Columbia University Press, 1956), 78.

4. On this methodological distinction see Lesslie Newbigin, *Foolishness to the Greeks: The Gospel and Western Culture* (Grand Rapids: Eerdmans, 1986).

5. Peter Enns, *Inspiration and Incarnation: Evangelicals and the Problem of the Old Testament* (Grand Rapids: Baker Academic, 2005), 23–67.

6. Kent Sparks provides a brief discussion of current views on the sources of the Pentateuch, *God's Word in Human Words: An Ecumenical Appropriation of Critical Biblical Scholarship* (Grand Rapids: Baker Academic, 2008), 82–88. A succinct explanation is in Norman Habel, *Literary Criticism of the Old Testament* (Philadelphia: Fortress Press, 1971); and a fuller explanation of Old Testament sources is in James Atwell, *The Sources of the Old Testament: A Guide to the Religious Thought of the Hebrew Bible* (London: T. & T. Clark, 2004).

7. For recent discussion of how narrative relates to testimony and history in the Gospels, see Martin Hengel, "Eyewitness Memory and the Writing of the Gospels," in *The Written Gospel*, ed. Markus Bockmuehl and Donald A. Hagner (Cambridge: Cambridge University Press, 2005), 70–96; and, Richard Bauckham, *Jesus and the Eyewitnesses: The Gospels as Eyewitness Testimony* (Grand Rapids: Eerdmans, 2006).

8. This is not to say there was not some editing and arranging of material, nor that there are no variant readings among the manuscripts. Most introductions to the New Testament discuss these issues.

Chapter Eight

Collections

THE YOUNG PERSON in this unit's case asked how the Bible came to be as it is; that is, how and why these particular books were included in the canon of Christian Scriptures.

Again and again I have met people who accept as a matter of faith that the Bible was delivered to us as it is. They may not be interested in how the Bible arrived at its present form. They even may be surprised that it is a topic. On the other hand, for many Christians the process of the Bible's formation is important because the process tells us something not only about the nature of the Bible but also about the way God communicates with us.

In the last chapter I explored how individual books of the Bible came to be as they are. In this chapter we will discuss the collecting of those books into the Bible as a whole. In order to do this, I must introduce the term *canon* and say more about tradition.

Canon

The word *canon* comes to English from Latin and Greek. The first definition of *canon* in the *Oxford English Dictionary* is "a rule, law or decree of the Church, especially a rule laid down by an ecclesiastical Council." The fourth definition is "the collection or list of books of the Bible accepted by the Church as genuine and inspired."[1] I acknowledged in chapter 5 that when early Christian writers referred to Scripture they meant the Hebrew Scriptures. The canon of Hebrew Scriptures was fairly intact by the Rabbinical Council of Jamnia in 90 C.E.[2] It is important to keep in mind, however, that the documents that were formally included among the Hebrew Scriptures already were considered sacred by the Jewish community. They were not made sacred by their inclusion, so much as they were included because they already were revered as sacred.[3] These were the writings that expressed and shaped the imagination — and with it, the faith and life — of the Jewish people and preserved their identity as God's chosen people.

The Church discovered very early in its history the importance of safeguarding the content of the apostolic message. In the second century after Christ's death and resurrection, the last of the apostles had died, the threat of persecution was growing, and questions were being raised about the sometimes scandalous content of the Hebrew Scriptures. Heretics and orthodox Christians alike used the Hebrew Scriptures to defend themselves. In this environment the Church was hard pressed to stabilize the authentic message of the Gospel. It did this in two interrelated ways: by clarifying the traditions of the apostles, and by collecting and preserving the writings that the apostles and their followers had handed down to them.

As with the Hebrew Scriptures, so too the writings included in the Christian canon were considered sacred by Christians long before they were formally canonized by a Church council.

Among the Christian leaders of the churches of the first several centuries, "canon" applied to more than the Hebrew and Christian Scriptures alone. It referred to the core faith of the apostles. Irenaeus, who was the bishop of Lyons, France, called this core faith the "canon of truth."[4] According to Irenaeus, this core faith had been handed on from bishop to bishop from the time of the apostles. Early Christians discerned the true Scriptures according to their compatibility with the apostolic faith, which they knew in part through the writings they honored as sacred. The process of deciding which documents would be included in the canon of Holy Scripture relied greatly on tradition. Just as tradition was integral to the development of many biblical documents, it was also integral to the process of collecting those documents into a canon of authoritative witnesses through which faithful witness was born to God's self-revelation in Jesus Christ.

Scripture and Tradition

The idea of authoritative tradition is in the Bible itself. The Greek word for tradition, *paradosés* (Latin, *tradere*), and related words are used in the Christian Testament. In 1 Corinthians 11:23, Paul recalls the Corinthians to the reverence they should have for the Lord's Supper. He writes, "For I received from the Lord what I also handed on to you...." J. N. D. Kelly reminds us that tradition's "authoritative delivery was originally to the fore and always remained prominent."[5] Roman Catholic and Eastern Orthodox theologians, among others, see the Eucharist as bearer of the heart of the Christian tradition.

The preservation of the memory of God's faithfulness was crucial to the life of the children of Israel from very early in their history. In Deuteronomy we have testimony to this emphasis: "You shall put these words of mine in your heart and soul, and you shall bind them as a sign on your hand, and fix them as an emblem on your forehead. Teach them to your children, talking about them when you are at home and when you are away, when you lie down and when you rise. Write them on the doorposts of your house and on your gates..." (11:18–20). In 2 Kings 22 we read how in the time of Josiah workers in the temple recovered the Scroll of the Law. The fact that the king led the people in public repentance for their forgetfulness is another indication of the emphasis on preserving the testimony to God's will and work in Jewish tradition.

Brevard Childs believes the evidence points to the biblical texts and the canon developing as one process. The essence of the New Testament canon is the living product of the early churches' pursuit of clarity about the Christian message or kerygma (Greek, meaning "proclamation") and the beliefs that attended it. The composition and editing of the documents of the New Testament were shaped by this canonical agenda. Tradition as the passing on and securing of sacred memory is essential to the identity of Judeo-Christian people. Childs believes that the Bible should be interpreted in this light.[6]

Determining the authentic apostolic witness would have been less complicated had the ancient lists of sacred texts been identical from Church to Church. There were varying traditions surrounding some of the books, which contributed to differences among the lists of honored Scriptures. The texts eventually gathered into the Christian Testament were part of the wider, living tradition of the testimony of the apostles, evidenced by the use of the writings in worship and baptismal preparation.

Tradition, then, was symbiotic, so to speak, with the written apostolic testimony. Together they attested to the truth about the person and work of Jesus Christ. This organic interrelationship between the apostolic writings and the tradition of the Church's witness was obvious to the early Christians. The texts that were identified as inspired and authoritative were identified as such because of traditions concerning their apostolic origins and their didactic or inspirational value, measured with reference to the rule of faith, which, as I said, the documents themselves helped to shape. It was a dialectical relationship: tradition confirmed Scripture and informed its interpretation; Scripture shaped tradition and anchored the Church's discernment of the authentic from the inauthentic among new movements and teachings.

Criteria for Inclusion

The chief criterion for including a document in the Christian canon was the belief that it was written by one of the apostles or his followers. The term *apostle* did not necessarily refer to the original twelve alone; the early Church also had in mind at least James, the brother of the Lord, Barnabas, and Paul.

Some documents were more readily accepted into the canon than others. Those "signed" by an apostle, with content reflecting the apostle's known teaching, already were in effect canonized by the churches' uses of them. Reasons to exclude a document from the canon included uncertain authorship, tension with the accepted apostolic message, and regional rather than general acceptance of a book's apostolic origin. This explains why Hermas's *Shepherd,* the *Apocalypse of Peter,* and the *Didache,* among others, were excluded from the canon even though they were widely considered to be edifying writings. Among those that were doubted early on in some sectors but eventually were included in the canon were James, Hebrews, 2 Peter, 2 and 3 John, Jude, and the Revelation of Jesus Christ to Saint John.[7]

Many documents were excluded from the Bible and from the devotional life of the Church because their contents were at odds with apostolic witnesses. The Gnostic writings so recently brought to popular attention by Dan Brown's novel *The Da Vinci Code* and by the high-profile publication of *The Gospel of Judas* are noteworthy examples of writings containing stories and teachings that are contrary to the earlier apostolic witnesses. (The Gnostic literature also was written later than most of the books finally included in the Christian Scriptures.)

Key Moments in Scriptural Canon History

As might be expected, there were pivotal moments on the road to finally establishing the canon. According to J. N. D. Kelly, "The earliest... catalogue of [Christian Scriptures] for which we have evidence" is dated to the second century and "recognized the whole New Testament except Hebrews, 1 and 2 Peter, James and 3 John."[8] It also included the apocryphal book of Wisdom. The fragment of this list dates roughly from the period of history when Marcion challenged the authenticity of the apostolic witnesses (mid-second-century C.E.).

Marcion was from Sinopē, which was in what is now called Italy. He saw such a difference between the God of judgment and wrath revealed in the Hebrew Scriptures and the God of love who was the father of our Lord Jesus Christ that he decided they must be two different gods. He regarded the latter as the greater of the two. In order to discern the authentic witness to the true God, Marcion looked for the God of love and forgiveness. He included in his canon only the writings in which he saw unequivocally and uniformly the God of love. With this hermeneutical scalpel, Marcion cut away much of what others considered sacred writing. The result was a greatly reduced set of authorized Scriptures containing only select parts of our present Christian testament.

Marcion's teachings had awakened the mainstream Church to the need for an authoritative body of writings. The Church rejected Marcion's belief in a lesser god superseded by the one true God who was the father of Jesus Christ, affirming instead that God was genuinely revealed Godself through the Hebrew people as we saw in chapter 5. The Hebrew Scriptures always had been authoritative for Christians. The Church recognized that it was and is through the Hebrew Scriptures that Christians discern who Jesus of Nazareth was and what he came to do. Had not the prophets pointed to him? Did not Abraham "rejoice to see [Christ's] day"? (John 8:56). Our understanding of God and God's creating, saving, and re-creating work would be greatly impoverished without the Hebrew Scriptures.[9] This was the first pivotal moment in the formalization of the Christian canon of Scriptures.

It was Irenaeus (late second century C.E.) who took Marcion's idea of a canon of authoritative texts and connected it with what he called "the canon of truth."[10] After Irenaeus came the great Christian scholar Origen of Alexandria (ca. 184–254 C.E.). It sometimes is said that Origen was the first Bible scholar in the modern sense of the word. He struggled with the relationship between the wisdom of the philosophers and the truth and wisdom of the Scriptures. Origen considered most of the Christian Testament that we know to be Scripture, though, according to Neill Lightfoot, he was "hesitant" about "Hebrews, James, 2 Peter, 2 and 3 John."[11]

By the time of Athanasius (ca. 293–373), patriarch of Alexandria and defender of the faith articulated at the Council of Nicea in 325 C.E., the extent of the Christian canon was fairly well clarified. In his Easter letter of 367 C.E.[12] Athanasius listed the texts of the Christian Scriptures as they are for us today.

Another influential moment in the early history of the canon was the rise of Montanism in the second century. I will save discussion of that for the next chapter, since the issues that movement raised pertaining to the Holy Scriptures have much to do with the work of the Holy Spirit in the ongoing development of Christian thought.

By the late second century, the core of the Hebrew Scriptures and by far the larger portion of the Christian Scriptures were well established as canonical. Though some questioning continued, controversy about individual books of the Bible largely subsided until the Protestant Reformation, when biblical theological thinking led Luther to apply the

Gospel as the standard for discerning true Scripture. (The status of the Apocrypha was another issue, which we do not have time to address.) In the end, Luther embraced the whole of the Christian canon, even the infamous "straw epistle" of James. (He had a difficult time seeing the Gospel in it.) Luther's critical thinking was part of a shift in worldview that had enormous consequences for the relationships among Scripture, tradition, reason, and experience.

Back to the Question

How and why did the Church include the writings that are in the canon of Christian Scriptures? The Church needed a canon of Scriptures to stabilize the truth about Jesus, his mission, and his purpose for the Church. The writings they chose were among the books already widely looked to by Christians as embodying the ongoing witness of the churches that had been founded by the apostles and their followers. The Church believed that the apostles or their immediate followers had written the writings they included.

The process of canonization and the extent of the accepted texts were and are not as clear as we might like them to be; but neither are these as vague as some may wish they were. The canon of Scriptures developed through a living process. This should not surprise us, since God shepherds us through life, respecting and using our humanness, glorifying Godself and us in the process and its outcomes.

Summary

The Church discovered very early in its history the importance of safeguarding the contents of the original message by committing the apostolic testimony to writing in the Gospels and by preserving some of the letters of the Apostles and, perhaps, their closest disciples.

The gathering of accepted documents into a single set of authoritative books for the faith and life of the Church is what we refer to when we use the term *canonization*.

The process of canonization had tradition at its heart. Scripture and tradition were and are related dialectically.

Some documents were more immediately accepted than others; some eventually were not included. The criteria for inclusion were apostolic sources, general use in the churches, and consistency of content with the rule of faith.

There were historic milestones in the long process of arriving at our Christian canon of Scriptures. Once established, this set of sacred texts became the principal measure of truth claims made by and for the Church until the Enlightenment, when other standards of authority became more pronounced in church and society.

Questions for Discussion

- Have you ever wondered why some books were included in the Bible? Are there any that you might like to call "straw," as Luther did the Epistle of James? What criteria do you employ when you decide whether to embrace their authority?

- How does the fact that some books in the Bible likely were not written by the author to which they have been ascribed either by tradition or signature influence your confidence in their inspiration and authority? Increase it? Undermine it? Why?

- Does the fact that the early Christians struggled to discern whether or not some books of the Bible should be included in the canon surprise you? Why or why not?

- Find a Bible that contains the Apocrypha. Compare its contents with the Bible. How is it similar? How is it different?

- Why should the canon be open? Why should it be closed?

Notes

1. *Oxford English Dictionary*, 1933, 1961, s.v. "Canon."

2. Neil R. Lightfoot, *How We Got the Bible* (New York: MJF Books, 1963, 2003), 154; "The canon was fixed long before Jamnia." See also Jack P. Lewis, "Jamnia Revisited," *The Canon Debate*, ed. Lee Martin MacDonald and James A. Sanders (Peabody, Mass.: Hendrickson Publishers, 2002), 146–162.

3. Lightfoot, *How We Got the Bible*, 162; Everett Ferguson, "Factors Leading to the Selection and Close of the New Testament Canon," in *The Canon Debate*, ed. Lee Macdonald and James A. Sanders (Peabody, Mass.: Hendrickson, 2002), 295.

4. Hans Von Campenhausen, *The Formation of the Christian Canon*, trans., J. A. Baker (Minneapolis: Fortress Press, 1968, 1997), 207.

5. J. N. D. Kelly, *Early Christian Doctrines* (London: T. & T. Clark, 1960, 1978), 30.

6. Brevard S. Childs, *The New Testament as Canon: An Introduction* (Minneapolis: Fortress Press, 1984).

7. Kelly, *Early Christian Doctrines*, 56–60; Shira Lander, "The Formation of the Biblical canon (s)," in *Scripture: An Ecumenical Introduction to the Bible and its Interpretation*, ed. M. Gorman (Peabody, Mass.: Hendrickson Publishers, 2005), 110–12; and several essays in MacDonald and Sanders, *The Canon Debate*.

8. Kelly, *Early Christian Doctrines*, 59.

9. Von Campenhausen, *The Formation of the Christian Canon*, 207: "The spaciousness which Marcion's dogmatism had obstructed has, thanks to Irenaeus, become a basic feature of the New Testament, never to be lost again."

10. Ibid., 186.

11. Lightfoot, *How We Got the Bible*, 158.

12. Ibid., 159.

Chapter Nine

Authority

I EXPLAINED in the last chapter that there was a crisis regarding the Hebrew Scriptures in the churches of the second century. People continued to be perplexed by the behavior of the God described in some texts there. (Just read the book of Numbers for plentiful examples.) We saw that Marcion's controversy had to do with authentic sources. Consequently, the churches clarified the status of the Hebrew Scriptures and began to formalize a canon of Christian Scriptures.

It was later in the second century C.E. that the Montanists troubled the mainstream of the churches. The Montanists pursued forms of spiritual giftedness that they read about in some of the writings of the apostles and their followers. They went too far in their emphasis on the Spirit. They believed that, since the Holy Spirit gifted them, their revelations superseded those that came before them.

Today, some Charismatic or Pentecostal Christians can be compared to the Montanists. They promote experiences such as "speaking in tongues" and receiving messages "from the Lord" and claim the gift of prophecy. Pentecostal and Charismatic Christians echo Montanist concerns and emphases; sometimes, but not always, they echo Montanist extremism as well.

New movements of the Spirit raise questions. Might new manifestations of the Spirit add to or correct what the Spirit said to Christians in the past? Might they even correct the Scriptures? If the Spirit is leading the Church, then what is the status of the continuing development of the Christian traditions, compared with the Scriptures? In our day, this question is broadened to include knowledge that comes to us "from below": science and history. How shall we weigh these sources compared with the weight we ascribe to Scripture?

Phases of Beliefs; Changing Worldviews

I have said from the beginning of this book that the Bible is the principal source for Christian knowledge of God and God's will. But apart from this basic affirmation of the Bible's central role, the churches' beliefs about the Bible have not been without change. In recent centuries questions have arisen about the nature of the Bible and the relationship of God to the witness its writers bear to God's will and work in the world. When explaining very generally these changing beliefs and the approaches to interpretations that reflect them, philosophers and theologians frequently refer to three overlapping and intersecting periods: the pre modern, modern, and postmodern. With each of these there came a change in the way biblical inspiration and authority have been understood.

Kinds of Authority

In graduate school I was the residence director of a dormitory. One day I noticed on a resident's car a bumper sticker that read, "Question authority!" I wondered if I were among the authorities she wanted to question; then I realized she had more important authorities, I might say "bigger fish," than her R.D. in mind. The authorities she questioned were more foundational to our society and culture.

What authorities have you questioned? Perhaps you have asked what kind of authority the churches claim for the Bible, or whether the Bible really should be an authority for faith and life.

The word *authority* is defined by the *Oxford English Dictionary* as the "power or right to enforce obedience; moral or legal supremacy; the right to command or give an ultimate decision." Further, authority is "derived or delegated power."[1] In other words, human authority is derived from a source beyond ourselves. The Church and the Bible are not exceptions to this fact. The shifts in views of biblical authority that occurred in recent centuries have to do with differences over whose meaning we find in it.

Premodern Faith[2]

Do you remember Heraclitus's river? He was the Greek philosopher who said we cannot step into the same river twice. Don't we grow weary of constant change? Like most of us, early Christians longed for permanence and security. They looked for stable meaning that they could rely on in the changing circumstances of life.

What could be more permanent than something of eternal value? Premodern biblical exegetes believed that God, the creator and sustainer of all that is, came to us in Christ Jesus and abides with us through the Holy Spirit, who communicates with us through the Scriptures.

A foundational belief about the Bible among premodern Christians was that the authors of the Bible were inspired by God to write as they did. Ancient and medieval Christians believed the biblical writers were led by God to bear witness to and to interpret God's actions in the world. It is not that they did not question the biblical texts, nor that they were unaware of many of the problems those texts presented. But they believed, nevertheless, that God was speaking to them through what the biblical authors wrote. Premodern Christians believed, in general, that God was the transcendent source of the Bible's meaning. They believed God was, in a meaningful sense, the author of the Bible.

The doctrine of the Incarnation was key to their understanding of Scripture. This is seen at least as early as Origen of Alexandria.

Spirit and Letter, Allegory and Event

Origen was a Christian scholar who lived in the late second and early third centuries. He was troubled, as many of us are today, by some of what he read in the Scriptures. God is said to have commanded the Israelites to do some heinous things en route to and in their life in the Promised Land. Origen believed that God inspired the entire Bible and that its words are mysteriously related to Christ as the transcendent and Incarnate Word, so he looked for meaning beyond the obvious in the words and phrases of the Bible. Beginning with the "literal" or "fleshly" sense, he practiced a way of interpreting the biblical writings that uncovered layers of meaning that were deeper and more profound than the plain sense. That deeper meaning was the spiritual meaning.

Origen's belief in the spiritual meaning of biblical texts was rooted in the platonic way of seeing the world. Plato believed that what is visible in the world is a reflection of the ideal form of it, which is beyond time and history. The spiritual was more real than the earthly or physical. In this light, Origen felt justified in teaching that there were three levels to biblical understanding: the fleshly, the psychological, and the spiritual. It is the spiritual sense that enabled the forms of figurative interpretation he so greatly treasured.

This figurative sense includes typology and allegory. Origen's interpretation of the Song of Songs is a classic example of looking for the deeper, spiritual meaning. The Song of Songs is a love song, rich with sensual imagery. However, Origen said the imagery of the Song stands for the relationship between God and Israel, and he made creative associations among texts in light of this allegorical connection. (Such allegorical interpretations are still heard in preaching.)

This method continued through the medieval centuries. The great Catholic scholar Thomas Aquinas taught a fourfold sense of Scripture, and in the sixteenth century Luther wrote that the romantic relationship that is celebrated in the Song of Songs stands for Christ and the Church.

None of this would be possible without assumptions about reality and meaning in relation to texts and their interpretations. The early Christian mind had no problem with the notion of humans receiving meaning "from above." Their worldview did not reflexively resist the supernatural. They believed that God is self-revealing in particular ways, including in the words of the Bible. They believed that the Bible, though comprised of many books and narratives, was a unified whole in the service of the story of stories — God's story. From this basis they were able to make the interpretive moves they did.

The Bible's authority was, for the premoderns, transcendent and divine. Their emphasis was on God as the divine inspirer of human authors. Modernity, which is the intellectual and social culture surrounding modern ways of thinking, brings humanity to center stage in biblical scholarship, just as it does in philosophy, art, and literature.

Modern Faith

In order to understand the modern period, we must consider the Enlightenment and the shift in worldview that it embodied. The Enlightenment was the eighteenth-century movement in European intellectual history marked by confidence in human reason and a celebration of human value and abilities in general. With this confidence came a willingness to question inherited assumptions and to critique earlier conclusions. The Enlightenment contributed to the rise of the modern period.

Moderns emphasize verifiable, empirical methods for testing truth claims, so the modern period has been marked by a questioning of traditional authorities. Moderns want to be able to see, touch, feel, or otherwise sense objectively what they call "true." For example, if I see that paper catches fire every time it is exposed to flame, I have justified the statement: paper is flammable. The truth of this statement can be demonstrated over and over. Moderns believe the universe is ordered and there are universally valid truths that their methods are designed to seek.

Among the inherited assumptions that cannot be verified is the idea that there is a God and, more to our point, that God was behind the Bible. (Our discussion of Kant in chapter 1 helped us to see this.) In the modern period, then, there was a shift in focus away from God as the source of meaning in the Bible and guider of the interpretation of the text. As I have said, this shift arose in part from renewed confidence in human reason to understand and to solve the dilemmas of human existence. Philosophical, linguistic, social, and methodological movements conspired to call into question historic assumptions about the relationship of Church, its book, and its traditions, to divine initiative. The modern gaze shifted from revelation from above to revelation from below, from the transcendent spiritual to the immanent material.

Exegetical methods reflected this change. Questions about authorship and increasing recognition that many biblical texts developed over long periods of time led to an emphasis on the text as such. Since the metaphysical (what is beyond the senses, which includes all things spiritual) cannot be verified, the effort was now to determine what the text meant in its time and place.

Modern approaches fall under the heading of "biblical criticism." (Criticism in this sense is not necessarily negative or skeptical. I will talk more about this in chapter 11.) Modern approaches have to do with getting at the human sources and, by better understanding them in time and place, locating the original meaning of the text. Here would be found the single, stable, objective meaning that the human mind craves, with supportive data and arguments that are respectable to a modern worldview for defending the preferred interpretation.[3]

Postmodern

The modern reader approaches the Bible by seeking meaning in author and text. In contrast, the postmodern attitude toward the Bible sees getting in touch with the author's intended meaning as impossible. The postmodern locates the source of meaning in the reader as the reader exists in community. The text has no stable meaning and there is no transcendent source of meaning. The postmodern interpreter is not as interested in an event as in a narrative's meaning for the interpreter. The Bible's authority is in the attitude of individuals and communities toward it; the local community determines valid interpretation.

A Qualifier

It is very important to emphasize that these terms — premodern, modern, and postmodern — are not necessarily tied to chronological periods of time. For example, the modernist point of view has not been universal among Christians in the modern period. Indeed, a long history of movements for and against modernism dots the theological landscape. For this reason, I must qualify what I said earlier. While I say that premoderns,

moderns, and postmoderns have characteristic philosophies and theologies that mark trends over time, I must acknowledge that all three approaches are embraced by Christians in our own day. The presence of fundamentalist, charismatic, and Pentecostal churches is evidence that aspects of premodern worldviews not only survive but are broadly appealing. Likewise, modern beliefs and attitudes are alive and well alongside postmodern Western culture. A diminishing of the mandate of the text's claim on the reader, measured in terms of the Bible's authority and the location of a stable meaning, is the essence of the change toward the postmodern.

The Incarnational Model

Over time, the perception of human subjectivity in interpretation has been growing. Some say postmodernity is ripe for reacquiring theological hermeneutics and the incarnational theology of Scripture in particular.[4]

My understanding of the Incarnation is classical, which is to say that I base my beliefs about Christ on the Council of Chalcedon (451 C.E.). Seeing Scripture as analogous to this understanding of the Incarnation enables me to embrace the human agency of God's involvement in the world. Here finally we may turn to a more thorough exploration of the incarnational model and its implications for hermeneutics and methods of biblical interpretation. It is to interpretation that we turn in the fourth and final part of our journey. These will be the final threads in the tapestry I have been weaving. You will have noticed, imaginatively, of course, that no matter how we look at it, this tapestry has Christ Jesus at its center.

Back to Our Question

What have Christians past and present believed about the authority of the Bible?

Until the modern period, influenced as it has been by the Enlightenment, the Bible was associated with God, and its authority was based on the belief that the Holy Spirit had superintended the formation of the Bible. With the shift in the modern period toward a more scientific worldview, the divine authority of the Scriptures gave way to increased skepticism. Where the Bible's authority survived, it was as a reflection of an affirmation that there is a remarkable connection between the very human authors and things divine. By locating meaning in readers and their communities, some expressions of postmodernity have taken skepticism to an extreme. Elements of earlier thinking and approaches remain in the periods that succeed them.

Summary

Early Christian conflicts over the canon and the role of the Holy Spirit challenged the Church to clarify where Christians may listen for God's authentic Word.

The authority of the Bible originally was derived from God as the perceived source of its meaning. The perceived loci of biblical truths shifted from above to below, from the premodern to the modern and then to the postmodern period of hermeneutic theory and practice.

Premodern Christians focused on the meaning of the Bible as what God intended to convey through the biblical writings by way of inspired human authors who were, nevertheless, real people in very human contexts.

Modern Christians are methodologically preoccupied. They see the Bible as data and the texts as having singular meanings that may be uncovered through refined techniques.

Postmodern Christians doubt that the authors' intentions or meanings can be discovered through texts, since texts mean something different to everyone who reads them. So the meaning of the Bible must be what readers make of it when they play by the interpretive rules of the community where they worship.

Methods of interpretation reflect worldviews. A worldview that rejects what may not be empirically verified will find it difficult to find transcendent meaning in biblical texts. A worldview that embraces God's transcendence and God's immanence in the Incarnation of God the

Eternally Begotten helps us make more sense of many of the difficulties we have been observing.

Questions for Discussion

♦ In what ways do you consult the Bible for guidance in Christian life and thought? What other sources do you consult when making decisions? What kinds of questions lead you to the Bible?

♦ Do you call the Bible God's Word? If so, why? If not, why not?

♦ Listen for typological or allegorical interpretation in the sermons you hear. Why do you think the preacher used allegory instead of focusing on "the plain sense" of the text?

♦ How does your worldview influence the way you see the Bible and how you interpret it?

♦ In what ways are your views of Scriptural inspiration and authority in line with the premoderns, the moderns, or the postmoderns? Why do you believe as you do about the Bible?

Further Reading

Davis, Ellen F., and Richard B. Hays, eds. *The Art of Reading Scripture.* Grand Rapids: Eerdmans, 2003.

Hall, Christopher A. *Reading Scripture with the Church Fathers.* Downers Grove, Ill.: InterVarsity Press, 1998.

Lightfoot, Neil R. *How We Got the Bible.* Grand Rapids: Baker Book House, 1963.

Metzger, Bruce M. *The Early Versions of the New Testament: Their Origin, Transmission, and Limitations.* Oxford: Clarendon Press, 1977.

Sparks, Kent. *God's Word in Human Words: An Ecumenical Appropriation of Critical Biblical Scholarship.* Grand Rapids: Baker Academic, 2008.

Von Campenhausen, Hans. *The Formation of the Christian Bible.* Trans., J. A. Baker. Minneapolis: Fortress Press, 1968, 1997.

Williams, D. H. *Evangelicals and Tradition: The Formative Influence of the Early Church.* Evangelical Resourcement. Grand Rapids: Baker Academic, 2005.

Notes

1. *Shorter Oxford English Dictionary,* 1933, s.v. "authority."

2. I am relying especially on Michael Gorman, ed., *Scripture: An Ecumenical Introduction to the Bible and Its Interpretation* (Peabody, Mass.: Hendrickson Publishers, 20005); and Justin Holcomb, ed., part 1 of *Christian Theologies of Scripture: An Introduction* (New York: New York University Press, 2006), among others for this survey.

3. Lesslie Newbigin, *Foolishness to the Greeks: The Gospel and Western Culture* (Grand Rapids: Eerdmans, 1986).

4. An exceptional effort toward this end is the set of essays in Ellen Davis and Richard Hays, eds., *The Art of Reading Scripture* (Grand Rapids: Eerdmans, 2003). Another is Jens Zimmerman's *Recovering Theological Hermeneutics: An Incarnational Trinitarian Theory of Language* (Grand Rapids: Baker Academic, 2004).

Part IV

Interpretation

Case Study: What Happened to Dinosaurs?

A teenager comes to you, the pastor of the Church the young person attends, to talk about something that is troubling her. She is studying dinosaurs in public school. At the same time, her Church school lessons are on the creation stories in the biblical book of Genesis. The young person's public school teacher and her Church school teacher have very different points of view about dinosaurs.

The public school teacher's explanation of how dinosaurs came to exist does not include God. The teacher says dinosaurs, along with many other kinds of creatures, had their time on earth many millions of years ago. Some evolved into new kinds of creatures; others ceased to exist because they failed to adapt. The teacher explained that, in the case of the dinosaurs, debate continues about what caused their extinction. There are those who say that some species that exist today are descendants of some of the dinosaurs.

The Church school teacher, on the other hand, teaches that God created the heavens and the earth in six twenty-four hour days. When the young person asked why dinosaurs were not mentioned in the creation stories, the teacher responded that the Leviathan mentioned elsewhere in the Bible may refer to dinosaurs. When the student pressed the question further, the teacher responded that the creation story in the Bible is not that detailed and that what is important to know is that God created everything and that God did it "just as the Bible says" — in six days.

Chapter Ten

Incarnation

I N OUR CASE, the young person's struggle reflects the tension in our society and within our churches about how we think the universe came to be. There are deeper issues at stake, though, evidenced by frequent energetic discussions on the subject. The deeper issues include: How does the biblical worldview relate to the modern? What may we expect to learn from the Bible: science, theology, or both? Does the Bible contain "factual" information about nature and the details of history?

The ways we answer these questions reflect our beliefs about God and the world. Our theology and the worldview that goes with it are inextricably linked with how we interpret the Bible.

The Two Core Doctrines of Christian Faith

I have said from the beginning of this book that the doctrine of the Incarnation enables us to understand how God shepherded the writers, editors, and compilers of the Bible so that they would produce the book of witnesses to the interaction of God with humanity, the book through which God speaks most clearly to all times and places. I also have pointed to relationships as at the heart of life's meaning and purpose.

In the first sermon I ever preached, I said that the main theme of the Bible is relationships. We see this in the first three chapters of Genesis, in which relationships are established and then broken: vertical relationships between God and humanity, horizontal relationships among humans, and existential relationships within humans. The main theme of the biblical narratives is about how God reestablishes relationships with us and among us. The Incarnation, Crucifixion, and Resurrection are the climactic chapter of the drama. Now we are moving toward the conclusion, when all will be fulfilled as Christ brings history to its proper end in us, for us, and through us.

This main theme — this meta-narrative, or grand story — was reinforced for me several years ago while I was talking with someone in the café at Palmer Theological Seminary, where I teach. I was chomping at the bit to get on with what seemed to be more important tasks when that infamous still, small, inner voice of conviction posed the question: What do you really value? What really is of lasting value? Then I remembered Christ, and gave thanks to God for the gift of ordinary conversations about mundane things. The deep sense of centeredness that I felt in the presence of the recognition of the Spirit's blessing on such moments of community has stayed with me. Life is about community. Relationships are the most enduring treasures of life.

I stand by that first sermon and the lesson in that much more recent experience: God loves community, because, though God is one, God is three. God is community. How could it be otherwise, since God is love?

The Holy Trinity

The doctrine of the Incarnation walks hand in hand with the doctrine of the Trinity. Indeed, it was the Church's recognition of Jesus Christ's divinity and humanity that provoked the thinking that recognized God as Trinity. Together, the doctrines of the Trinity and of the Incarnation are the dynamic center of Christian theology.

As the early Christians tried to understand the life and work of Jesus Christ, they concluded that they saw God the Creator in the teaching and actions of the man Jesus of Nazareth. The Holy Spirit, like Christ, behaved as one who has personhood.[1] This raised the crucial question: If the Father, the Son, and the Holy Spirit all are God, and yet they are distinct personae in their own right,[2] how are Christians to make sense of monotheism? The belief that there is only one God is the very heart of Judaism. How could God be one and be three with such personal identities at the same time? These questions are understandable; we continue to wrestle with them.

The effort of the early Church was to embrace the mystery that had been revealed while trying also to make reasonable sense of it. Though not unanimous, the conclusion that has endured is that God is three and yet also one, one and yet three, unity in diversity, diversity in unity, perfect community of being, the Holy Trinity.

Many theologians — myself included — believe that knowing God as Trinity helps us to see that God created us in order to share with us the perfect community of being that God is in God's own being.[3] This conclusion has been reinforced by an ancient analogy, expressed through the Greek word *perichoresis*, that recently has been reclaimed by Protestant theologians. (There is no perfect analogy for the Trinity in this world; nevertheless, there are echoes of the Trinity in creation.)[4]

The word *perichoresis* describes the Trinity as an "interpenetrating community of being." Its etymology, though, is more revealing. The root is *chor*, as in choreography, the art of designing a dance. The prefix *peri*, as in *periscope* and *perimeter*, means "around." *Perichoresis*, then, literally means "dancing around."[5]

Each persona of the perichoretic Trinity dances to a unique step in the Divine Dance. No one persona of the Trinity has the same steps as the others; none can dance their own steps without the others; and each shares in the others' dances without actually doing what the other does. The dance they do is one dance about which they are in perfect concert.

One example of this is the birth of Christ. God the Eternally Begotten became the Incarnate Son in the womb of the virgin Mary, by the work of the Holy Spirit, in accordance with the will of God the Father-Creator. A second example is the crucifixion of Jesus Christ. Jesus was on the cross by the will of the Father and able to endure in the power of the Spirit, but it was Jesus himself who suffered and died. Each has a proper work that is that persona's own, but each shares in the works of the others. They do nothing alone. The proper work of the Father (Parent) is to create; the proper work of the Son (the Eternally Begotten) is to redeem. But what is, then, the proper work of the Spirit? What is the Holy Spirit's step in the dance?

The Spirit and Community

The Spirit's work is to apply and enable the work of the Son. Thomas C. Oden puts it this way: "The sequence of salvation proceeds from the benevolence of God the Father toward humanity, through the atoning death of the Son in offering redemption, toward the grace of the Spirit in applying and enabling redemption. The whole triune God works toward salvation."[6]

The second chapter of Acts tells of the coming of the Holy Spirit in power on Christ's disciples. It was the Spirit who birthed them into the fellowship of God and one another, which Jesus had prayed for: "that they may be one, as we [God and Jesus] are one" (see John 17:11, 22). The goal of the Spirit's work is community: community formed by God, community in the manner of heaven.

You see, then, how the doctrine of the Trinity provides us with a thoroughly relational way of understanding God. Revelation is dialogical because it is about relationships! When Jesus walked among humanity, that dialogue was quite literally happening in and through Christ, the truly human and truly divine Savior.

Incarnation

I will not repeat here what I wrote in chapter 3, where I discussed the Incarnation; however, there is more that needs saying.

In addition to what we find in the beginning of the Gospel of John (the divine Word "became flesh and lived among us"), deep early Christian thinking about Jesus Christ is seen in the great *kenosis* hymn in Philippians (*kenosis* is the Greek word for an emptying). Paul writes, "Let this mind be in you that was in Christ Jesus, who though he was in the form of God, did not regard equality with God a thing to be exploited, but emptied himself, taking the form of a slave, being found in human likeness. And being found in human form, he humbled himself and became obedient to the point of death even death on a cross" (2:5–8). In Colossians (1:15–20) there is another hymn, this one to the preexistent Christ. It begins: "He is the image of the invisible God, the firstborn of all creation; for in him all things in heaven and on earth were created, things visible and invisible, whether thrones or dominions or rulers or powers — all things have been created through him and for him." The first epistle ascribed to John begins with an assertion of a firsthand encounter with Christ's physical humanity: "We declare to you what was from the beginning, what we have heard, what we have seen with our eyes, what we have looked at and touched with our hands concerning the word of life" (1:1).

These texts present both sides of the early Church's twofold witness to Jesus Christ: his humanity and his divinity. Some early attempts at explaining the relationships between these two aspects of Jesus Christ's person were rejected by the Church for compromising one or the other. The earliest were the Ebionites and the Docetists; in fact, 1 John is largely a response (or a reaction) to Docetism (see 1 John 4:1–3).

At the root of the word Docetism is the Greek word δοκεο, which means "I appear." The Docetists believed God could not really become a human because humanity is changeable and subject to physical and moral corruption. They believed Christ only *appeared* to be a human being, but was completely divine. The Church rejected Docetism because the Christ to which the Apostles testified was manifestly human; furthermore, only by really becoming a human being could Christ have saved us.

According to the Ebionites, on the other hand, Christ was fully human, but not really divine. The Ebionites believed Jesus was manifestly a human, but, since God could not become a human being and remain God, Christ must have been adopted into divine sonship at his baptism. The Church objected. It said the Gospels demonstrate that Jesus Christ was not merely human; he manifested divine attributes, and furthermore, he must have been divine to save us.

There were many variations on what came to be called "the two natures controversy" in Christology. (Christology is the study of the nature, character, and actions of Jesus. Expressed more broadly, it is careful thinking about who Jesus was and what he came to do. Christological thinking is foundational for Christian identity.) As noted earlier, the Church affirmed at the earliest ecumenical councils[7] that Christ was truly human and truly divine.

How does this way of thinking about the two natures of Christ help us understand the problem of the divine inspiration and obvious human character of the Scriptures?

The Bible as Revelation

We in the churches have been sorely tempted, especially in the two erroneous directions that first appeared with the Docetists and the Ebionites. Docetist and Ebionite Christologies parallel erroneous ways of understanding God's relationship to Scripture.

Think back to chapter 6. Verbal plenary inspiration of Scripture is a Docetist point of view; general inspiration is an Ebionite perspective. Applying to the Bible the early Church's logic for balancing its Christology enables us to avoid Docetism and Ebionitism (objectivism and subjectivism) in our view of the Bible and in our ways of interpreting it. (This requires the kind of dialectical thinking I explained in chapter 3.)

Consider a Bible passage connected with our case study. Chapter 3 of the book of Genesis tells the story of the fall of Adam and Eve. When you read that story, do you think of an actual garden, an actual speaking serpent, and God really walking step-by-step in the Garden of Eden? Or, do you think it is not historical but rather a story that tells a truth that applies to all humanity? The first response is an objective, Docetist way of interpreting the text; the second is a subjective, Ebionite way of interpreting the text. The Docetist does not recognize the story's history or its genre; the Bible is divine and therefore to be believed as it is. The Ebionite interpretation sees the Bible as merely human; it sees Genesis 3 as having no history behind it — merely a metaphor for human struggle with sin and no more than that.

Implications of Incarnational Inspiration

Classic Christology informs an incarnational view of the Bible that translates into a balanced view of its inspiration, authority, and a similarly balanced way of interpreting it. A point-by-point analysis follows.

Revelation is not primarily about objective content as such, nor about religious feelings alone. It is about meeting God in person through the transhistorical conversation of the communion of saints with and around the Bible.

The incarnational view understands that all Scripture is inspired by God in the sense that God stirred and shepherded all who wrote, edited, and compiled it. To say that one part of Scripture is the result of God's stirring and another is not exposes us to arbitrary and selective use of the Bible.

We incarnationalists are plenarists of a sort. We are not, however, verbal plenarists. We do not believe God guided the word choices of the writers and editors of Holy Scripture. So we avoid Docetism, which compromises the humanness of the Bible. We also avoid Ebionitism, since we believe the whole Bible is theologically and ethically trustworthy when interpreted contextually in light of the great story of God's love and salvation, judgment and mercy.

We incarnationalists believe that all Scripture is inspired by God, but all Scripture is also human. The texts express the humanity of their authors, including life experiences and contexts. The long, complicated process that resulted in the Bible teaches us something in and of itself. We learn from it that God does not override the personhood of the people God chooses in order to communicate with us. Through them, in their contexts, we learn how they met God in their time and place. The Word spoke through human beings in a way that respected their humanity, just as the Incarnation respected the human being whom God the Eternally Begotten became.

Looking at the other side of the coin, those through whom God spoke — with their authorial intentions, the limitations of language, and the conditioning of cultures — did not impede the divine purposes for their inspiration, just as the humanity of Jesus did not compromise the divinity of the Word made flesh.

We may be called "varied inspirationists" in that we believe not all Scripture is inspired in the same way or for the same purpose. The landscape of Scriptural inspiration is uneven, as indicated by the variety of genres in the Bible. God did not move in the same way or for the same purpose on all occasions, but God's great purpose was always operative.

We believe Scripture is authoritative, but the authority borne by one text varies from another because authority is related to purpose. This is determined according to genre and immediate theological intention. A poetic text that declares the glory of God as Creator is not authoritative for understanding the manner in which God created.

The incarnational view of the Bible denies that the Bible contains developed doctrine as such. The two bedrock doctrines we have been discussing are cases in point. The teaching that God was incarnate in Christ and that God is three and yet one are in Scripture to be discerned; but much dialogue, grounded in Scripture and tradition, was necessary to arrive at these reasonable and coherent doctrines.

For Barth, the Bible was not God's Word; rather, it bears God's Word. The incarnational model, strictly speaking, affirms that the Bible both is and bears God's Word, singular; that is, it bears God's great message conveyed through so many and varied messages. Though I am affirming that the Bible may reasonably and legitimately be called God's Word because its words are uniquely related to Christ the Word, the words of the Bible are not God's own words. Luther described the Bible as "the cradle in which the Christ-child is laid." We must keep clearly in mind that the Bible is only the penultimate expression of God's speech.

We cannot go so far as to call Scripture divine in an ontological sense. Keeping this distinction firmly in mind helps us resist the problem of reversing the analogy of the Incarnation. Jesus Christ is not like Scripture.

Through Scripture, the Spirit continues to bear witness to the truth of God in the person of Jesus the Christ and to bring us into personal relationship with God. The type of knowing that we may expect to experience through the Bible is relational; it is in community that we learn the truth about God. I believe God's intention for the Bible is to testify to and to anchor the continuing dialogue between God our Creator and humanity. Just as God shepherded the Bible's formation, the Holy Spirit stirs our interpretations of it, as we seek God's guidance in faith.

Back to Our Questions

What kind of knowledge does Scripture provide? The writings of the Bible do not bear scientific knowledge or reportorial history as such. The Bible was written from particular times and places with worldviews of their own; the truth the Bible bears is borne through those contexts with their attending worldviews. The knowledge the Bible bears is relational.[8]

How may we listen for the Spirit through these texts? It is to methods for good listening that we turn next.

Summary

We cannot fully appreciate the doctrine of the Incarnation unless we understand the doctrine of the Trinity. The doctrine of the Trinity points us to God's intention to bring us into community with Godself and with each other. Communication is essential to this communion.

The Incarnation demonstrates that God uses earthy means below to communicate objective transcendent truth from above. Christ Jesus was uniquely the ontological incarnation of the Divine Word of God. The Holy Scriptures approximate, but do not achieve, incarnational reality. They are very human and very divine; but they are not, in fact, the Divine Word.

This has implications for the way we understand the Bible's nature and how we interpret it. On the one hand, we may say that transcendent truth may be known through the Bible; on the other hand, we must admit that we see but "through a glass darkly." The Bible does not contain fully developed doctrine, but doctrine may be gleaned by the communities of God's people seeking to know God more and to serve God better in dialogue with God through it.

All Scripture is inspired by God, but inspiration can vary. God did not violate the humanity of those who wrote and edited the Scriptures, nor does their humanness prevent God from accomplishing the purposes for which the revelation was given. All Scripture is authoritative, but in different ways for different purposes.

The Holy Spirit shepherded the Scriptures and continues to speak God's Word through them. Revelation comes from above through the full participation of what is below. While the whole of the Bible is God's Word — or message — the words are not God's words; while the words are not God's own words, God's Spirit uses these words to express God's Word.

Questions for Discussion

♦ What do you think of *kenosis* Christology? What do you think Jesus Christ knew, let us say, at eight years of age? What do you believe Mary and Joseph taught Jesus?

♦ Did Jesus make mistakes as a boy and later as a carpenter? What is the difference between failing at a mundane task and failing morally?

♦ Do you believe there are scientific and historical errors in the Bible?

  – If you do, does this undermine your belief that God speaks through the Scriptures?

  – If you do not, how do you reconcile what we know about the physical world today with the stories in the Bible?

♦ What would be the characteristics of a human community in the image of God's perfect community of being?

Notes

1. Not only the Son, but the Spirit too was declared to be "*homoousios* [of one and the same substance and being] with the Father." T. F. Torrance, *The Trinitarian Faith: The Evangelical Theology of the Ancient Catholic Church* (London: T. & T. Clark, 2000), 195.

2. As I said above, I prefer *persona/ae* because it does not imply individual human persons, and yet it suggests personal distinction.

3. Stanley Grenz, *Theology for the Community of God* (Grand Rapids: Eerdmans, 1999).

4. Augustine, *De Trinitate*, saw in human experience, made as we are in the image of the God, analogies to the Trinity.

5. Shirley Guthrie, *Always Being Reformed: Christian Faith for Today* (Louisville: Westminster John Knox, 1996), 40.

6. Thomas C. Oden, *Systematic Theology: Life in the Spirit*, vol. 3 (San Francisco: HarperSanFrancisco, 1994), 25.

7. *Oxford Dictionary of the Christian Church*, rev. 2nd ed., ed. F. L. Cross and E. A. Livingstone (Oxford: University Press, 1958, 1983), 443. "The whole inhabited earth" is the etymological meaning of the Greek word from which our word *ecumenical* comes. The great councils were called ecumenical because all the bishops from "the inhabited earth," were invited to attend.

8. Relational knowledge necessarily has ethical implications.

Chapter Eleven

Methods

THE YOUNG PERSON in our case has been taught to interpret Genesis on the basis of assumptions about the Bible that are difficult to sustain in light of what I have covered in this book. She has been taught that it is possible to take the entire Bible literally and still make sense of it. It is no surprise that she might struggle with the statues of Genesis vis-à-vis scientific discoveries.

The real problem behind her dilemma is that her view of God's inspiration of the Bible is not consistent with what we know about the history of the Bible or with what science has demonstrated to be factual about the universe. She has been taught to interpret the Bible in a way that has led to conclusions, supposedly based on Scripture, that conflict with modern science.

In this chapter I will explain in greater detail, but still briefly, the methods of biblical interpretation that respond to these principal questions: What methods of interpretation correlate with an incarnational theology of Scripture? What methods convey biblical faith for our day? What methods discern a biblical theological view of the world without perpetuating a view that conflicts with what we know about the world? We have space only to establish a general sketch of these methods in this chapter.

Premodern Interpretation

Premodern imagination was (and is) more directly formed by the biblical vision of the world than is the more recent imaginative life of secular Western societies. In the literature of ancient writers we can see that there are differences between what people believed was real then and what we in the Western world believe is real today. These differences, though, can be overstated. Early Christians were not as uncritical as many of us moderns and postmoderns are prone to think. The great Christian thinker and scholar Origen of Alexandria, whom I introduced in chapter 8, was honest about the problems he saw in the Scriptures; some of those are problems we also see. Like many of us, he held to his belief in their divine inspiration even while taking his questions about the Bible seriously. As we saw earlier, Origen's solution was the figurative method of interpretation. For Origen and many other ancient practitioners of figurative interpretation, biblical texts had more than one legitimate possible meaning. (In this sense they were akin to postmoderns.) Their figurative interpretive methods were allegory and typology.

Figurative Interpretation

Early Christians acknowledged and generally respected the "plain sense" of Scripture (its most immediate and obvious meaning), but they did not think biblical passages had only one meaning. With only a few exceptions (the Church at Antioch resisted allegorizing), they felt free to employ typological and allegorical interpretation. They did not believe, however, that biblical passages had an infinite range of meanings. For Origen, Christ governed the perimeter of possible interpretations.[1] The focus of the premodern, Western European imagination was God, so they looked for God's meaning in the Bible.

Though both allegory and typology are figurative, which is to say that both see meaning and significance beyond the plain sense of the Bible, there are important differences between them.

The root of the word *typology* is the Greek word *typos*, meaning "pattern, example, model, [or] standard."[2] The typological interpreter looks at events in the past, for instance, and sees foreshadowing of and preparation for events to come. This approach is careful to sustain a direct correlation between the events in the biblical text that it connects.

For example, the story of the near sacrifice of Isaac by his father Abraham can be interpreted typologically. According to this typology,

God required Abraham to sacrifice his son Isaac to prove his own faithfulness to God. But before the deed was done, God stopped Abraham and provided a ram to sacrifice instead. One typological interpretation sees Abraham as a type, or model, of faithful humanity, and the ram God provided was a type of Christ. The "historical" story points to what came later: Christ sacrificed himself in our place.[3]

Allegory takes figurative interpretation further from the historical meaning and context of the passage. Unlike typology, allegory is not necessarily bound by what was said to have happened; indeed, allegorical interpretation may be so far removed from the event that the earlier narrative and context cease to be meaningful for the interpretation derived from it. In extreme allegorizing, the narrative of the biblical text serves merely as a launching place for the imagination rather than narrative grounding for interpretation.

Figurative interpretations were acceptable, and even preferred, during the Middle Ages. Openness to multiple levels of meaning, along with differences of worldview and criteria for verifying truth claims, are among the chief differences between premodern and modern beliefs about the Bible and how to interpret it.

Just the Facts, Please

The focus of the modern imagination was (and is) humanity. The modern imagination therefore seeks the human meaning in the Bible.

Modern developments in epistemology favored inductive methods of verification with a preference for fact. Questions and doubts about the factuality of the Bible led to efforts to salvage universally applicable truth and wisdom from it. Emmanuel Kant and Friedrich Schleiermacher (1768–1834), who is commonly regarded to have been the father of modern theology, are notable thinkers in this regard. In particular, the question of the real life and teachings of Jesus, compared with the stories of the life and teachings of Jesus as presented in the Gospels, preoccupied many discussions among biblical scholars. Their thought and methods have had a lasting impact on biblical studies.

George Eldon Ladd wrote helpfully about these methods. His clear discussion of several forms of biblical criticism guides what follows here.[4] (Keep in mind that "criticism" in this context refers to the systematic study of the texts; it does not imply an effort to undermine the texts, though that is certainly a possible consequence of criticism.)

Types of Criticism

Text criticism attempts to discern the most probable forms of the original manuscripts of the Scriptures. No such original manuscripts are extant, so text critics use linguistic tools to examine the inconsistencies and variants (for instance, a story that appears in one manuscript and not in another) in the earliest manuscripts and translations that do exist. It is important to get as close to the original forms of the manuscripts as is possible. Textual critics provide this invaluable service.

Literary criticism attends to problems in translation as such. Literary critics clarify meanings and grammatical structures by looking at many uses of a given word or phrase throughout the history of a language. The meanings of words are dynamic; they have histories and they continue to evolve. Some words are impossible to translate accurately from one language to another. Literary critics help us find the best words in our languages for translating the words and phrases from ancient biblical times, places, and languages.

Form criticism reflects the clash between premodern and modern worldviews more than other types of criticism. It was developed by scholars who doubted the miracle stories and divine claims of Jesus presented in the Gospels because they had no evidence of miracles happening in modern times. They concluded that the miracle stories in the Gospels were added after Christ was crucified. Form criticism looks for evidence of the oral traditions on which the Gospels are based and tries to distinguish between the historical Jesus and the Jesus of the Church's early, developing faith.

Redaction criticism takes the methods of form criticism a step further. It examines how literary sources were utilized by the Gospel writers in ways that express their own and their communities' theological beliefs.

Like form criticism, redaction criticism distinguishes the Jesus of history from the Christ of faith proclaimed by the Church; however, unlike form critics, redaction critics seek and value the theological points of view of the editors who shaped the books we have.

Finally, **historical criticism** looks at the events, customs, way of life, and so on, at the time of the composition of the Scriptures. Knowledge of these may correct or enrich our interpretations. For example, the Apostle Paul's reference to the citizens of heaven (Eph. 2:19) is susceptible to misunderstanding because the experience of citizenship in Paul's society was much different than in ours. Hence, a study of Roman citizenship promotes sound interpretation.

These contextual differences, among other factors, provoke the skepticism of postmodern thinkers about the possibility of universal meaning. Skepticism has become more intense with the arrival of postmodern philosophy and theology. And we have come back to where we started with the case at the beginning of this book: "All is relative!"

Postmodern Interpretation

As I said in chapter 9, the essence of postmodern thinking about the meaning of what we read in general and of the Bible in particular is that readers and their communities determine the meanings of texts. The postmodern imaginative shift focuses on the self and the self's community. This is why postmodern thinkers will not easily admit universal truths.

So religious texts that have shaped worldviews are not accepted as authoritative in themselves; rather, it is the readers' interpretations of them that are authoritative, and that only in their own communities. This results in a leveling of interpretations: all are equally valid; no community has the right to insist that other communities see the world as they do. Such insistences are disguised power plays.

Not all postmoderns have been willing to sacrifice all forms of transcultural, even theologically transcendent, meaning. Narrative theologians have argued that all people are storied people; that is, stories shape who we are and what we believe.[5] Our stories are life-shaping, and life shapes our stories. Some go further, saying that every story is part of God's great story. It is the stories of the Hebrew people and God seeking and relating to them and their relating to each other that we have in the Hebrew Scriptures. The same is true of the Christian Testament: God's story is the key to the meaning of every story, and, according to the Christian faith, God's story with us is centered in the Incarnation.[6]

This thinking has spawned yet another kind of biblical criticism: *narrative criticism.* This approach examines the biblical text with the same methods used by literary critics of other kinds of literature. While this arena of methods, as applied to the Bible, does not eschew the effort to understand biblical passages in light of their ancient contexts (as in historical criticism), its focus is on the unitary form of the text that we have before us.

Related to narrative criticism is *reader response criticism.* These methods are concerned with the effect of the text on the reader. It asks, What is the position of the text in relation to the reader? And how does that influence interpretation.[7]

Incarnational Interpretation

How, then, does incarnational interpretation look? What form does it take?

All methods proceed from presuppositions. Modern and postmodern methods, despite their differences, both take the humanity of Scripture seriously. Incarnational interpretation appreciates this fully, but also takes absolutely seriously our faith that God has attended, and continues to uniquely attend, to the Bible. I have been employing the biblical image of shepherding as complementary to the incarnational analogy for Scriptural inspiration. A shepherd does not control. A shepherd guides.

Proceeding with the faith that God the Spirit is in the world and uniquely speaking to us through the Bible when it is faithfully and contextually interpreted, we are able to see and to receive the hope and meaning God provides through it. By faith we are open to the shepherding inspiration of the Holy Spirit, and the Bible becomes for us the

Word that is "a lamp unto our feet and a light unto [our] path" (Ps. 119:105, KJV).

When guided by the Holy Spirit, our humanness serves rather than compromises God's purposes. Since the humanity and the divine inspiration of the writers and editors of the Bible are fully embraced in this view, both texts and contexts must be fully explored in biblical exegesis. Critical methods help us to understand the humanity of the Scriptures, but they must be used in faith: faith in God's will and purpose to use the Scriptures and our interactions with them for our sake. Since God's purpose for the Bible is to cultivate the community of God's people, our interpretations finally must occur in our communities of faithful seekers, and we must be conscious of the influence of our own cultural heritage on our interpretations.

All together, the incarnational model helps us to be comfortable with dynamic, rather than definitive, levels of confidence in our interpretations. We do not demand precision or objectivity where it cannot be; but we look for it, nonetheless. We see subjectivity as problematic only when it is celebrated at the expense of the reasonableness of faith; indeed, we welcome interpersonal subjectivity as enabling the inspiration that God offers through the Spirit; but we recognize that love invites us to press into knowing better and better the One into whose community we are being invited.

It will be helpful to have a set of questions that reflect the incarnational view of the Bible to guide our interpretations. I will begin chapter 12 with a sequenced list of the questions I am recommending.

Summary

The question posed via our case was, what methods of biblical interpretation correlate with an incarnational view of the Bible? In order to address this question we surveyed several methods that arose in connection with premodern, modern, and postmodern ways of thinking about the world. Premoderns looked to God's meaning and had no trouble believing there is a grand narrative or story that permeates the Bible. Modern thinking looked for humanity's meaning in the text. An emphasis on factuality led to a search for singular and universal truths in the texts, seen in their contexts. Critical methods served this agenda. Postmodern interpreters have confined our gaze not only to earth, but to very particular local communities. Out of these, they say, universals cannot be insisted on from community to community. The best that can be hoped for is shared wisdom through shared stories.

In light of the incarnational view of Scripture, more relational methods are in order: methods that promote dialogue and community in the presence of a text that finally stands over us because God the Holy Spirit speaks uniquely through it.

Questions for Discussion

◆ When you read the Bible, do you imagine that God is speaking to you personally through it? Or do you imagine that the authors of the Scriptures are speaking and that they have something to say that God is using?

◆ How do you interpret the Bible? What is your "method of interpretation"?

◆ Do your methods of interpretation get in the way of your encountering God, or do they help you encounter God through the Bible? Do you encounter other Christians through the Bible?

◆ What understanding of the nature of the Bible is expressed through your approach? Do your methods appreciate the humanity of Scripture? Do they honor the divine inspiration of the Bible?

◆ Think about the stories of Creation and Fall in Genesis 1–3: How would incarnationalists interpret those stories? What might the image of the speaking serpent represent?

Notes

1. Justin Holcomb, ed., part 1 of *Christian Theologies of Scripture: An Introduction* (New York: New York University Press, 2006), 11–80.

2. UBS, Greek New Testament, Dictionary: 185.

3. John Chrysostom, "Homilies on Hebrews," no. 25, book 2, *Nicene and Post-Nicene Fathers*, series 2, vol. 15 (Peabody, Mass.: Hendrickson Publishers, 1887, 1994), 478–79.

4. George Eldon Ladd, *The New Testament and Criticism* (Grand Rapids: Eerdmans, 1967).

5. Alister McGrath, *A Passion for Truth: The Intellectual Coherence of Evangelicalism* (Downers Grove, Ill.: InterVarsity Press, 1996), 105–17. George Lindbeck, *The Nature of Doctrine: Religion and Theology in a Postliberal Age* (Philadelphia: Westminster Press, 1984). Hans Frei, *The Eclipse of Biblical Narrative: A Study in Eighteenth- and Nineteenth-Century Hermeneutics* (New Haven, Conn.: Yale University Press, 1974)

6. I am using story and narrative interchangeably for convenience' sake in this short work; see Richard Bauckham, "Reading Scripture as a Coherent Story," in *The Art of Reading Scripture*, ed. Ellen F. Davis and Richard B. Hays (Grand Rapids: Eerdmans, 2003), 43.

7. James L. Resseguie, *Narrative Criticism of the New Testament: An Introduction* (Grand Rapids: Baker Academic, 2005), 17–40.

Chapter Twelve

Application

OUR TASK IN THIS CHAPTER is to apply a method of interpretation to a particular passage that relates to at least one of the issues I mentioned in the introduction to this book. Given the scriptural focus of our case study, it may surprise you that I have chosen John 1:1–18, rather than Genesis 1–3. There are at least three reasons for choosing John 1. First, the issue that relates to the case study at the beginning of this section (Part IV) of this book is creation, and John 1 is indirectly about that. Second, this passage is well suited for demonstrating the method I am recommending in a way that relates to the issue of creation without bogging us down in the technical considerations that come with Genesis 1–3. Third, John 1 is about the Incarnation of the Word of God in Jesus Christ, and that is, as you know, the doctrine that is nearest to the heartbeat of this book.

Our Guiding Questions

We will investigate the passage by systematically answering a series of questions that engage the text both exegetically and hermeneutically.[1] The substance here is provided by commentaries representing sound scholarship across a range of points of view. They provide access to the wisdom and insight of those who spend a lifetime studying the Bible. Through commentaries we are also able to consult the wider body of Christ and learn wisdom that may call us beyond the boundaries of our local communities. Such commentaries will help us answer our questions.[2]

1. What are the passage's boundaries? Where does it begin and end?

Though there is a natural break in the flow of John's narrative where the beautifully written identification of Jesus as the preexisting Divine Word, now Incarnate, ends, the identification of Jesus as the Lamb of God by John the Baptizer completes the identification of Jesus. It is not until after Jesus' baptism by John that Jesus begins to gather disciples. That is the beginning of his ministry. The passage, therefore, may be demarcated as beginning at 1:1 and ending at 1:34, where John passes the prophetic mantle onto "the Son of God."

2. Are there significant differences among the major translations of the passage? If so, how are they significant?[3]

I compared the New Revised Standard Version of the Bible with two other translations, Today's New International Version and the New Century Version. There are several issues in translation worthy of discussion, but I will deal with just one of them here, verses eleven and twelve.

> TNIV: [11]He came to that which was his own, but his own did not receive him. [12]Yet to all who did receive him, to those who believed in his name, he gave the right to become children of God—

> NRSV: [11]He came to what was his own, and his own people did not accept him. [12]But to all who received him, who believed in his name, he gave power to become children of God,

> NCV: [11]He came to the world that was his own, but his own people did not accept him. [12]But to all who did accept him and believe in him he gave the right to become children of God.

It is not exactly clear based on these two verses alone whether Jesus came to the Jewish people or to humanity as a whole. John says simply "his own" and "his own people." The translators of the NCV try to clear up the ambiguity by considering the broader theological context of this passage. They insert "world": "He came to the world that was his own." ("The world" is not in the Greek text.) The other two translations let the ambiguity stand, leaving the reader to discuss the reference more precisely by way of context.

3. What is my first response to the passage? Do I have a "gut level" reaction to it? Does it provoke questions? For example: Does it seem disconnected from the modern world? Is God's behavior in the passage other than I would expect?

Reference to the divine Word seems abstract until the Gospel writer brings "flesh" and "dwelling among us" into our frame of vision. The interspersed comments on the Baptizer add to my sense that the very One who made all things has come to earth. This arrests my attention. I think it would grab the interest of any readers who reflect on questions of the ultimate meaning of life. The writer points to Jesus as the One who can answer life's questions and lead us to the better place we seek.

The questions this passage provokes for me relate to the age-old problem of the very idea that the divine Word became human. Many of us were taught to assume God has characteristics, or attributes, that seem irreconcilable with human limitations. The problem becomes especially acute for me when I think about God in Christ Jesus the human being — an infant, child, and teenager; an itinerant teacher with an exhausting ministry; a wrongfully convicted man dying on a cross. Surely he fell and scraped his knee; he needed his parents to teach him and care for him; he felt pain and cried out in anguish before he died. How does the idea of the *Lógos* in Greek thought really help us to understand Jesus? Might it get in the way of the Truth that was revealed in him — the Truth that Jesus Christ was revealed to be?

4. What is the literary context of the passage? Does it sound like something I have heard before? What is its genre? How does its genre help me understand its meaning?

According to Bible scholars, the Gospels are a unique literary genre. They do not fit exactly into any prior category of writing, which increases the challenges of interpretation. In addition, Matthew, Mark, and Luke see the life and work of Christ through similar lenses because they draw largely from the same sources. The Gospel of John, however, does not share these sources, and has a theological intentionality about it that has led many scholars to conclude that the author put the sequence, and perhaps the contents, of events in the service of what he wanted to say theologically about Jesus the Christ.

5. **What theology is being asserted in the passage? What truths about God and the original audience are assumed or being taught?**

Tradition places the distribution of the Gospel in Asia Minor (present-day Turkey). Many people in the Eastern Mediterranean region would have recognized the influence of Greek thinking in John's language. John identifies the *Lógos* as the personal God who created all that is. He adds theological content to the idea, and that transforms it. In Christ, the *Lógos* of God came in person to tell us and to show us God and the truth about us. More broadly, we may say that in Jesus Christ, who is identified here with the Word, meaning took on form and flesh (the human word). In flesh, the *Lógos* is the long-awaited Christ of the Jews, who came to "take away the sins of the world."

6. **What was going on at the time the passage was written or edited that might help us understand its meaning for its ancient audience?**

It was a guilty and pessimistic era. In addition to the idea of the *lógos*, the first chapter of the Gospel contains imagery that reflects the Church's confrontation with the Gnostics. At the probable time of the writing of this Gospel, Gnosticism was a widely pervasive influence in the eastern Roman world. Gnostics generally regarded the material world as the evil creation of a lesser god. The goal of life was to escape the vagaries of physical existence; so the idea that the divine light came into contact with flesh was abhorrent to them. I agree with the observation that John's identification of Jesus with the divine light is a corrective to the influence of Christian Gnostics.

To the Jewish people God is Holy. John the Baptizer's identification of Jesus the *Lógos* as the Christ integrates Hellenistic and Jewish themes.

7. How does it feel to try to walk through the passage in the shoes, so to speak, of the characters in it? What might it have meant to the original readers?

Jesus of Nazareth was the Word and the Light, says John. The significance of saying, in effect, that God always was like Jesus must be interpreted in light of the fatalism of the ancient world. The affirmation of the divinity of Christ Jesus is counter to that fatalism. The original audience in Greek-speaking Roman territory would have rejoiced, I believe, to hear that One who is greater than the fates had come to our aid. Jewish readers would have rejoiced to hear that, in Christ Jesus, God dealt decisively with their sin and guilt.

8. What meanings have other Christians, past and present, gleaned from it? Are any of the interpretations offered contrary to the meaning of the text as seen in its contexts?

There is fair unanimity among the translators of John 1:1: "In the beginning was the Word, and the Word was with God and the Word was God." The translators of the New World version of the Jehovah's Witnesses, however, dissent from this translation. They prefer, "and the Word was a god."

Suffice it to say here that there is a genuine ambiguity that must be resolved by looking not only at the direction the grammar leans, but also at the direction the theological context points to. The grammar leans toward "the Word was God" because the lack of an article attached to the word "God" in the original Greek helps us see that *"the Word,"* which has an article, is the subject. The absence of an article with "God," does not, then, necessarily imply "a." This alone does not decide the matter, but adding the theological context where the author clearly is establishing the deity of Christ as foundational to his Gospel renders "the Word was God" the obvious preference.

9. Are there other passages in the Scripture where the theme(s) in this one are visited?

Other Christological hymns in the Christian Scriptures would be especially worth exploring and comparing (see Col. 1:15–20 and Phil. 2:5–11). Genesis 1–3 obviously was in the mind of the author(s) when he wrote, "In the beginning was the Word." Note that John says who created us, which is what so many of us believe is the main point of Genesis 1–2. John also says that God has dealt with what has haunted us since the beginning (Genesis 3): sin and the guilt that attends it.

10. **What transformation of faith and life occurred, or did the author intend to occur, through this passage?**

I think the main desired change in the readers[4] likely was to establish or strengthen faith in Jesus Christ among Jews and Gentiles by making clear who he really was: the *Lógos* and the Christ. Another was to inoculate them against Gnostic associations of evil with the flesh and to provide hope in the face of the pessimism and fatalism of the time. Another was to address the problem of guilt by asserting that Jesus came to satisfy the demands of the Law.

Hermeneutic Questions

11. **What truths does the passage have for me, my community, and the world? What aspects of who I am and of the community where I live influence the way I am interpreting this text?**

We also live in an age that is flirting with Gnosticism and fatalism. Many continue to ask the questions, "Who was Jesus, really? What hope does he offer me and mine?" An untold number of answers compete for our allegiance, but John's main points still resonate today. There is no need to be pessimistic. Nothing but God has the power to control our eternal destiny, and God has come, "full of grace and truth." We need no longer be haunted by guilt. Though we are very small, in Christ God came to the very particular. He did not remain far off, but became "the lamb of God who takes away the sins of the World." That makes his work for all of us, including you and me. The past need not distort the present and the future.

12. Are there aspects of who I am and of the community where I live that influence the way I am interpreting this text?

There always are. I have studied Greco-Roman philosophy and live in a society where those ideas have been influential. I wonder what those who have not studied theology and philosophy first see in this Gospel and in this passage in particular. I wonder how people from cultures not influenced by Western philosophy hear this passage. I would like to know how a person who worships or reveres ancestors in Africa or Asia would interpret the *Lógos* becoming flesh.

13. How may God, through this text, transform or encourage the community of the body of Christ of which I am a part?

There are times when I wonder how many of us experience skepticism about whether there is a God, and if there is, whether that God is interested in us. The universe is unimaginably vast; we are not even microscopic compared with the whole of it. I enjoy science fiction, which frequently raises questions about ultimate meaning and sometimes offers answers that make me think that if they were true, there would be very little about day-to-day existence that would be meaningful. We need regular assurance that our Creator is interested in, and has a purpose for us on this little speck of dust at the edge of just one of the myriad galaxies in the universe. That is what the truth of this passage declares to me, and, I believe, to my community as well.

Much more could be said about this incredibly rich passage from the Fourth Gospel; just one more observation must be made. This passage is primary for the doctrine of the Incarnation. So it is here that we find the clue to how God reveals God's character and will that we have been working with throughout this book. Hence, the passage's meaning for us includes indirectly providing insight into how the Bible was inspired.

Questions for Discussion

◆ Do you agree or disagree with my interpretation of this passage? Why, or why not? How do your usual methods for interpreting the Bible compare with those I am recommending?

◆ How is your theology of the Bible evident in the way you interpret it?

◆ Reflect on how God speaks to you through this passage. In what ways are your reflections rooted in your culture? How do they help you to speak prophetically to your culture?

◆ Do you wish you could talk to me about my interpretations of this passage? Why, or why not? With what community do you study the Bible? Name the people you would like to invite to study this passage with you.

Recommended for Continued Study

Bartholomew, Craig G., and Michael W. Goheen. *The Drama of Scripture: Finding Our Place in the Biblical Story.* Grand Rapids: Baker Academic, 2004.

Brauch, Manfred. *Abusing Scripture: The Consequences of Misreading the Bible.* Downers Grove, Ill.: InterVarsity Press Academic, 2009.

Brown, Jeannine K. *Scripture as Communication: Introducing Biblical Hermeneutics.* Grand Rapids: Baker Academic, 2007.

Holgate, David, and Rachel Starr. *Biblical Hermeneutics.* London: SCM Press, 2006.

Jensen, Alexander S. *Theological Hermeneutics.* London: SCM Press, 2007.

Resseguie, James L. *Narrative Criticism of the New Testament: An Introduction.* Grand Rapids: Baker Academic, 2005.

Russell, Letty M., ed. *Feminist Interpretation of the Bible.* Philadelphia: Westminster Press, 1985.

Smith, James, K. A. *Speech and Theology: Language and the Logic of Incarnation.* New York: Routledge, 2002.

Zimmerman, Jens. *Recovering Theological Hermeneutics: An Incarnational Trinitarian Theory of Language.* Grand Rapids: Baker Academic, 2004.

Notes

1. Jeannine K. Brown, *Scripture as Communication: Introducing Biblical Hermeneutics* (Grand Rapids: Baker Academic, 2007), 139–273, thoroughly explores an interpretive methodology apt for an incarnational view of Scripture. After I wrote this chapter, I read and reviewed Manfred Brauch's *Abusing Scripture: The Consequences of Misreading the Bible* (Downers Grove, Ill.: InterVarsity Press Academic, 2009). Prof . Brauch expertly applies interpretive methods that correlate with an incarnational understanding of biblical inspiration to a range of debated current issues.

2. A range of perspectives is provided by the following easily accessible commentaries, which I consulted for this chapter: William Barclay, *The Gospel of John*, vol. 1, rev. ed., in the Daily Study Bible Series (Philadelphia: Westminster Press, 1975); R. V. G. Tasker, *John*, in the Tyndale New Testament Commentaries (Grand Rapids: Eerdmans, 1988); Gerard Sloyan, *John*, in Interpretation: A Bible Commentary for Preaching and Teaching (Louisville: John Knox, 1988). Ambitious interpreters might also look at the Expositor's Bible Commentaries, the Anchor Bible series, and the Interpreter's Bible commentaries.

3. Questions for those who know Greek include: Are there any challenges for translating the passage? If so, what is their significance? Are there any textual variants? In this passage, there are several variant readings, but the scholars who have edited the United Bible Society's Greek New Testament are quite confident that their choices represent the original manuscripts, so we need not discuss them here.

4. Kevin Vanhoozer, *Is There a Meaning in This Text: The Bible, the Reader, and the Morality of Literary Knowledge* (Grand Rapids: Zondervan, 1998), discusses the implications of speech-act theory for a canonical linguistic approach to hermeneutics.

Chapter Thirteen

Summary and Conclusion

Summary

THE BIBLE IS THE PRINCIPAL primary source for Christian faith and life. God inspired those who wrote and edited the Bible to bear witness to God's Word in action. Even though the Bible was written and edited by human beings, the Bible is where the Holy Spirit bears authoritative witness to God, who revealed Godself in person — in Jesus the Christ.

Inspiration is a transformative stirring of the inner person that happens in response to many possible sources. While all inspired creativity is both objective and subjective, some is more objective; some is more subjective. For example, books provide a more definitive word than paintings, so we Christians look to the Bible for authoritative guidance on how best to live.

Even though writing is a precise, or more objective, way of expressing the meaning a person is inspired to convey, it is not purely objective. The inspiration that comes from books raises questions about the intentions of authors, the uses of genres, the status of texts, and the life setting of the reader compared with those of the authors. These concerns reveal the very subjective dimensions of interpersonal communication. Knowledge of other persons must be both objective and subjective, if it is to be really interpersonal and really what we would call personal "knowing."

When we say the Bible is inspired by God, we mean that there is a unique relationship between God and the Bible. God shepherded the human authors and editors, as well as the Church as it formally recognized its canon of Scripture. God moved them in ways that changed them in their times and places and speaks prophetically to us as well.

131

Times and places are contexts. Biblical writers and editors responded to their contexts from within these contexts (how could they do otherwise?) and God respected them fully as human beings as God moved them to write from their transformed and transforming place of faith and life. What they had to say also spoke to their contexts in ways that shaped the further development of their communities — and ours.

The canon of Scriptures developed through a long dialogical process among witnesses, responders, editors, and compilers. Rarely can our understanding of the Bible's inspiration and authority depend on the inspiration of single authors. Tradition and Scripture quite simply are inseparably and dynamically interrelated. The crucial matter for the authority of Scripture is derived from God's work in relation to it — from our belief that God shepherded the very long and human process that produced the Bible.

God did not stop shepherding Scripture upon the clarification of the canon. Communication can be a challenge. (We are fallen and prone to self-deception. But that is another subject.) The problems of God's communicating to humans through language would be even greater if God did not continue to shepherd our interpretations of Scripture. The Holy Spirit weaves an ever dynamic and lively tapestry of faithfulness in and through the communities attending to the Scriptures as they bear witness to the Great Shepherd. It is through the Spirit's guidance that God's Word speaks through the Bible. In order for us to hear, we must have faith in God; we must trust God to communicate God's Word with us through the Holy Spirit.

Back to Drama

In contrast to the view that God takes total control of history and Scripture, seeing the nature of biblical inspiration as analogous to the Incarnation enables us to sustain a faithful and realistic view of the Bible, as well as balanced methods for interpreting it. It also enables us to account for the drama of life and of history.

History and the Bible breathe with the stuff of real drama.[1] Real drama is born of freedom, which produces relationality, and authentic relationships — community — are at the heart of drama. If we subtract the freedom of the authors and editors and assume that God exercises full control, we cannot account for the drama that is in the pages of the Bible. On the other hand, we cannot account for the dramas of life, let alone history and the Bible, if there is no plot, no grand narrative or story of which we all are a part; no meaningful path through crisis, climax, and resolution to promised conclusion.

The incarnational analogy for the Scriptures, and the related ways of interpreting them, helps us account for both the freedom and for the plot we see in Scripture. It accounts for the particulars and the whole, for the stories and the Great Story (the story God invites us to join).[2] It helps us comprehend the objective concreteness we bump up against when God speaks the Word of judgment, as well as our subjective experiences, without which there are no authentic relationships.[3] It helps us weave a thread of unity where the conflicting questions of our time would divide us, a thread that tempers our convictions with humility and grounds our humility on firm convictions. As we see and interpret the Bible incarnationally, God's Word comes again from above through the full and active participation of what is below, and the Spirit's work continues in our time, creating now, as the Spirit always has been creating, the community God intended, the community we are becoming, the community we shall be.

Notes

1. A major theologian who explored theology in dramatic and aesthetic terms was the Roman Catholic scholar Hans Urs von Balthasar. See also Kevin Vanhoozer, *The Drama of Doctrine: A Canonical Linguistic Approach to Christian Theology* (Louisville: Westminster John Knox, 2005).

2. N. T. Wright, *The Last Word* (San Francisco: HarperSanFrancisco, 2005), 115.

3. See chapter 1 above.